# REFLECTIONS IN MY MAGICAL MIRROR

## LESSONS OF LOVE FROM THE SCHOOL OF LIFE

### SPIRITUALITY 104

IVÁN FIGUEROA-OTERO, M.D.

# REFLECTIONS IN MY MAGICAL MIRROR

## LESSONS OF LOVE FROM THE SCHOOL OF LIFE

### SPIRITUALITY 104

MASCOT BOOKS

**www.mascotbooks.com**

***Spirituality 104: Lessons of Love from The School of Life***



www.ivanfigueroaoteromd.com

Editor and translator: Yasmín Rodríguez, The Writing Ghost, Inc.
www.thewritingghost.com

Cover design: Gil Acosta Design
www.gilacosta.com

All Bible quotes are from the New International Version (NIV), 2011 update.

Part of Dr. Figueroa's book series, School of Life

**For more information, please contact:**
Mascot Books
620 Herndon Parkway #320
Herndon, VA 20170
info@mascotbooks.com

Library of Congress Control Number: 2020911854

CPSIA Code: PRV0421A
ISBN-13: 978-1-64543-078-0

Printed in the United States

I dedicate this book to all teachers, students, and patients with whom I have participated in the School of Life, who inspired me to share all their experiences and lessons. I'm especially grateful to my patients who, with the testimonials of their lessons of love, helped me find the Key to Forgiveness to reach the soul's healing code. Without them, my academic advancement in the universal classroom would not have been possible.

If, while being reflected by this book's mirror, some of you rediscover your shadow-distorted light, share the merit of the results with your fellow students, as well as the learning that follows from reading it.

# REVIEWS

"The material in this book is a treasure, full of practical advice for us all. It is a great guide to start[ing] out our days with a quote and a thought to direct us toward all the positive behaviors we can create in our brain's laboratory."

*—Dr. Norman González Chacón, one of the founding fathers of natural medicine and the bioethical way of life*

"'The good man gives good things from his good treasure.' That quote from the Great Master describes, in essence, the type of person that is Dr. Iván Figueroa, who once more masterfully shares his treasure of knowledge through the Magical Mirror. This valuable book contains deeply profound thoughts that help us free ourselves from the limiting entrapment of the traditional world and open ourselves to new interdimensional doorways. The book teaches how to set ourselves free from the bindings of suffering and failure and to hope to love and be loved again, unconditionally. It is, therefore, the master key to open the iron bars wrapped around our emotions that sicken our soul."

*—Héctor Díaz Rodríguez, professor, University of Puerto Rico, Río Piedras Campus*

"This is my opinion about Dr. Figueroa's fourth book, a work of art that positions him as a proven author and a wise, mature teacher. His books complement his work in the spirituality knowledge area, just like his spirituality complements his vocation as a healer: this is the duality of knowledge.

The organization of the book in quotes is original and allows the reader to look into multiple mirrors, which are descriptions of the multiple dimensions of human existence. The quotes are also fragments of life's threads, valuable for readers of all ages.

This is a book about religion and psychology, reasoning and empiricism, science and poetry, psychological diagnosis and advice. It reflects what is learned in life when confronted with human pain in all its dimensions, causes, and contrasts; when you identify with the author's empathy as a doctor and a human being; and when Compassion is transformed into action through Charity (note the capital 'C').

The author works on, as in his other books, the inconsistency of reality's contrasts, demonstrating his knowledge of the Taoist dual vision. His holistic approach harmonizes science and spirit and what's modern with what's eternal; erases lines; and creates a universe with his Magical Mirror metaphor.

This is also an eminently practical book that doesn't only present general advice, but also specific techniques to achieve totality, peace, and Aristotelian fulfillment, slowly and with a lot of patience, perseverance, and discipline. Its emphasis on the act of forgiveness to disrobe oneself from destructive bindings, in the act of self-criticism or introspection to reach knowledge and in love as a method and a goal, is immensely valuable.

This book is a must for readers of all ages: easy to read, with profound knowledge and existential applications, a guide to life."

*—Dr. Eduardo Santiago-Delpín, immunologist and transplant surgeon, distinguished professor of the University of Puerto Rico*

"This book has music inside because it made my soul dance with the salsa of the Spirit."

*—Choco Orta, salsa singer and percussionist, actress, women's rights activist*

"Unamuno said that truth lives inside men. Coming from that perspective, we need to ask how to reach it. Dr. Iván Figueroa-Otero facilitates that search with his latest book: *Reflections in my Magical Mirror*. From his first writings, this author integrates the human body's health with the health of the soul and the spirit. He traces a holistic path of individual commitment where we confront the labyrinths of our fears, guilt, lack of self-forgiveness, and so many other toxic feelings that are detrimental to our mental and physical health.

This new book reminds us of our mirror, but not the Sartrean one, but one that looks back at us and talks to us, offering the knowledge to achieve a full life even in times of adversity or existential crisis. The book provides deep thinking and simple, concrete concepts to overcome the challenges we face from the outside, remembering to always turn to the inside since there resides the truth."

*—Professor Beatriz Rosado, director of the radio show "Investigando y Rebuscando" from Cadena Radio Universidad de Puerto Rico*

"Dr. Ivan Figueroa's book series and his most recent compilation of these important reflections remind us of the power of love to transform our lives and our work and our world around us. Only when we look into the Mirror can we see the reflection of our Creator and remember the great purpose of love which brought us into being. When we do all things with love, then and only then do we live our true life's purpose. Thank you, Dr. Ivan, for tracing this pathway and reminding us of whom and where we came from so we can be the change we want to see in our lives and our world."

*—Melissa Turner*

*co-founder and editor-in-chief,*

*BeMagazine.org*

# OTHER BOOKS BY THIS AUTHOR

***Spirituality 101:***

*For The Dropouts of the School of Life:*

*A Review for the Final Exam*

***Spirituality 1.2:***

*For The Disconnected From The School Of Life:*

*A Review for Tekkies*

***Spirituality 103:***

*The Forgiveness Code:*

*Finding the Light in Our Shadows*

# TABLE OF CONTENTS

# ACKNOWLEDGMENTS

Among all the travelers who have shared this endless journey in the reflection of the mind's magical mirror, I want to particularly thank my children, their mother, and my patient wife, Ivette, who have supported this old man's follies with so much affection.

I especially appreciate the spiritual guidance from my masters in the Nyingma Tibetan Buddhist tradition, the Venerable Khenchen Palden Sherab Rinpoche and Khenpo Tsewang Dongyal Rinpoche, from whom I learned a good portion of the mental training that allowed me to write about the wonderful wisdom of the Mirror of our minds.

I equally acknowledge the primordial influence that the six volumes of *El Ser Uno*

"Being One" (www.elserunobooks.com), channeled by its author/channeler (anonymous), had over this book.

Finally, my thanks to my mother, Doña Berta, for hours spent reading the Christian Bible to me during my childhood, assuring me that at some point it would strengthen me during the difficult times in my life.

"The Master is nothing more than a disciple, who likes to help others to find their mastery."

"The weapons of the true Warrior of Light are compassion and the patience to wait for the other person to learn what he has already learned."

"Don't respond with your Shadows to the Warrior of Shadows, respond with your Light so that he may discover his own."

*—Iván Figueroa-Otero, MD*

# POEM

"The Magic in My Mirror"

The magic of my mirror lies in the inclusivity
of its reflection,
just as its wisdom, like in a mirror,
was reflected in the beginning
of the great reflective explosion of love,
which was full of Creation's
magical intention.
Thus, it allowed its loving inclusivity
to completely bathe
every dimensional corner with its brilliance.
From here arises the great responsibility
to abide by
the infinite and consequent shades of
our decisions
that are the origin of emotional forces
distorted by ignorance.

They obscured the beautiful purity of our
original, inclusive image
reflected as mere shadows of their
original format.
The attachment born from the loss of our
inclusive, magical vision
gave birth to a new universe full of deformed
and exclusive shadows
created by our ego,
the false substitute for our Magical Mirror.
But the distorted memory of the
original brilliance
motivated us to scrutinize the darkness of
the shadows
imprisoned in the subconsciousness
of our mind,
the inclusive light of our original image.
During this courageous act we find the key
to decipher the light hidden under the gloom
created by our ignorance,
forgiveness,
allowing us to erase the imaginary shadows
to find the lessons of love

that returned inclusivity to the magical reflection of our mirrors.

# INTRODUCTION

At the end of our book trilogy, we must take a break and congratulate ourselves for a successful conclusion of the basic level of the curriculum for the School of Life. Also, we should get ready for the next level, which I'll offer in the upcoming book series. We must know by now who we are, where we come from, and where we are going. We must recognize the importance of our constant duality as the biological offspring of matter and the spiritual offspring of antimatter (spirit). We should also understand both experiences are simultaneous and holographically interwoven in a harmonious symphony of love, understanding, and compassion where the biology is spiritualized, and the spirit is humanized.

In our first book, *Spirituality 101: For the Dropouts of the School of Life: Review for the Final Exam*, we found a universe where students from all learning levels share the experience as if in a large classroom at the School of Life. Every test includes an individualized educational experience, even for when we fail, since the universe allows us to retake it until we learn our lesson of love. In this school, there are no dropouts—only those who stop retaking their tests.

In our second book, *Spirituality 1.2: For the Disconnected From the School of Life: A Review for Tekkies*, we adapt the religious/traditional message to be more technological and cybernetic, to help deliver the message efficiently to younger minds. Here, happiness depends on avoiding disconnections with the primordial universal programmer or data source, and not allowing any corruptions to the original software from a virus like selfishness and individualism. This corruption distorts the programmers' minds (browsers), making it so that navigating the cybernetic web of the universe is an inconsistent and disagreeable experience. The solution for this paradox is to update our software by reconnecting to the original program and removing the virus, since all suffering comes from the primordial software's corruption.

In the third book, *Spirituality 103: The Forgiveness Code: Finding the Light in Our Shadows,* we discuss our software's corruption in further detail with a psychological and spiritual vision. Here, guilt caused by the mistakes made in our past experiences, and the toxic emotions that come from that guilt, create fictitious distortions on the original image from our Magical Mirror (primordial mind). These distortions (shadows) create emotional battlefields where we, as warriors, self-inflict wounds (guilt) that trap us in mental prisons, full of suffering, where we cannot find happiness in our universal journey.

This last book, *Spirituality 104: Lessons of Love from the School of Life: Reflections in my Magical Mirror*, is a detailed review of all the lessons from the first three levels for those who read them. It is also a full summary for advanced students from other schools who want to join the next level class without reading the first books. After reading the quotes in book 104 and their explanations, the new students must decide if they will continue with the following levels or if they want to read the first books before continuing in our school system.

*Spirituality 104* showcases fifty-two quotes from the first three books. These quotes represent our mind's knowledge reflected in our mirrors, like a creative display that reminds us of the magic left in our hearts by the Creator. The detailed discussion included with each quote allows us to study and practice them as individual lessons, which prepares us for the next educational level of our universal school. The format allows for its use in weekly reading groups, where participants' testimonies add authenticity to the educational experience. As always, each discussion has exercises to practice the lesson of love hidden in each quote. Book 104 represents the transition from the hundreds trilogy to the two hundreds, which symbolizes the second phase in our multidimensional exploration to return to our origins.

The Magical Mirror symbolizes the primordial Creator's mind, which we usually call God, where creation happens in an instant, imaginary explosion of love. That explosion creates the mirrors (minds) in the image and likeness of God's offspring. These mirrors have the responsibility within their free will to discover and organize every creative manifestation of the Magical Mirror and to ensure it reflects the light and love of the Creator in every corner. But like we saw in the first levels, keeping our mirrors' reflections clean and pure is not as easy as we first thought.

It is my most sincere wish that these quotes fill any educational voids left after the first three levels, and that they motivate you to join the next phase of our return journey.

# QUOTE 1

*The middle way is a tortuous one, be patient.*

This quote, originally from the Buddhist philosophy, was developed to modify Hinduism's extreme philosophy, which classifies the universe in opposing polarities between material (impure) or spiritual (pure). Here, the process of spiritual development was directed towards the purification of the material attributes of the body, which inhibited a state of enlightenment. In reality, this created a system of yoga practices of extreme abstinence from any physical or mental action that, according to the practitioners of that era, was the only way to obtain the highest state of spiritual realization.

When Prince Gautama, or the Buddha, started to search for the significance of life's suffering, he used all the existing ascetic variants but failed to find the answers to his questions. One day, his excessive fasting almost killed him, but a maiden saved him by offering him water and "forbidden" food. When he accepted them, his body recuperated and his mind cleared up. In this new stage of his life, he started to meditate again. Tradition says one day he was close to a river's edge when he overheard a conversation between a music teacher and his disciple who were navigating the river's waters. The discussion led him to develop his Middle Way philosophy. The teacher, who wanted his disciple to master playing the lute, asked, "When does your instrument sound better—when you tune the strings too taut, or when you tune them loose?"

The student answered, "It sounds better when I tune the strings not too strongly or too loosely, but somewhere in the middle where it is right." Buddha, in his meditative state, understood that the mind, like the strings of the lute, must be at equilibrium according to the melody (experience) it wants to play at that moment. This is the basis for the teachings of the Middle Way.

I base my vision of the Middle Way in the oriental philosophies of Taoism and Buddhism, where all universal experiences are in a continually changing equilibrium. None of the variable manifestations are unnecessary or harmful since each one has an educational role for the collective benefit of all the entities sharing the experience. That is why in my third book, *Spirituality 103: The Forgiveness Code*, I share the following quote: "Shadows are only shades of Light, and Light is a shade of the Shadows," and "We need to learn how to find the Light hidden in our Shadows."

The Middle Way is a way to approach the detours in our chosen path without wasting much time and without losing sight of our final destination. Those tortuous alterations in our route—which sometimes feel like a disagreeable waste of time and other times feel like marvelous experiences—always end up extending the time it takes to reach our final destination. The Middle Way philosophy motivates us to take fewer detours and to use up less time when we do take a detour. It allows us to learn from every detour, good or bad, like a road map (patience), and to trace a more direct route to our goal.

## EXERCISES TO INTERNALIZE THE MESSAGE

Begin with the Meditation from the Colorful Bath of Love. (See References and Resources.)

Next, choose one happy experience and one sad experience from your life. Visualize them in detail and write down the emotions they provoke. Now, review all other experiences that were direct results from those first two, short and long-term, and observe if they resulted in different feelings from the original ones. Examples of experiences: a romantic relationship ending in heartbreak; the birth of a son or daughter; difficult obstacles during the upbringing of that son or daughter; a new job position that brought new challenges but also unexpected results. Observe how there are contrasting assessments of both good and bad experiences, but they all transform into lessons of love. Do you remember your disappointment when you reached some of your most important goals?

# QUOTE 2

*A smile in the shadows of sadness is like a lighthouse that guides us to the land of love.*

To explain this quote, I'll use my book about the origins of suffering, *Spirituality 103: The Forgiveness Code,* as a reference.

"The Warrior who does not understand where he comes from and who he is feels lost in an unending battle with time and change, created by his habits." This is a human being who does not recognize his spiritual origin as a son of God and believes only in his natural birth, with death as his only destiny. The son of God always knows where he came from and where he will go after death, but the son of man doesn't know if something happens after his natural death. The son of man is always afraid of dying, and this drives him to use up his time efficiently to look for things he thinks will provide happiness. Fear of death brings forth selfishness, the main reason for human suffering.

This personal search for gratification causes a discrepancy with other beings regarding what happiness really is. This is emphasized by this quote from one of my books: "The search for happiness is one of the few actions in which human beings absolutely agree, even if we don't concur in what it is and how to find it." Further clarification can be found in this other quote: "Living, if we do it selfishly and without conscience of our interdependence with the laws of the universe and other beings, turns into a nightmare full of suffering with brief moments of happiness."

The sadness in the discussed quote comes from the insatiable void of a soul thirsty for love that cannot be satisfied with egotistical, mundane sensations. Happiness must be a state of balance (well-being) in the mind that doesn't depend on what's going on outside of it.

The smile of a person who recognizes himself as a son of God is filled with the love that projects from his origin, very similar to a light from a lighthouse that projects hope to sailors lost in the emotional storms of their lives.

## EXERCISES TO INTERNALIZE THE MESSAGE

Begin with the Meditation of the Colorful Bath of Love. (See References and Resources.)

Remember the saddest moments in your life and what events helped you heal that sadness. Sometimes, these experiences came along with pleasant experiences that mitigated the tragic aspects. Sometimes, sharing our woes with others or reading books where others have remedied similar situations could alleviate the negative impact. A hug made in solidarity and a contagious smile could become the beginning of a healing process. Understanding that we have recovered from similar situations in the past is also another source of healing. Finally, it's worth recalling that our exact origin transcends the human experience and that every negative experience hides a lesson of love. Don't forget that with just a smile, we can all be like lighthouses for others if we recognize that the smile lives in our hearts.

# QUOTE 3

*Variable reflections in the mirrors (minds) of others are like those of a house of mirrors in the fair: they tend to confuse who we really are.*

To explore the significance of this quote, I will once again use my book, *Spirituality 103: The Forgiveness Code,* as a reference. In its glossary, I define the mirror as the human mind made with the image and likeness or the primordial consciousness. That's where God reflects his creative love in his Magical Mirror, from where the two minds originate: the transcendental mind (God, or anti-material) and the relative mind (man, or material). Both are manifestations of the conscience of the Warrior of Light and the Warrior of Shadows, respectively. This represents the potential state of the universal creative process that existed before the Big Bang. In my book, the mind (mirror) represents the vehicle or time machine that allows warriors to complete their creative, exploratory trip.

The minds of the explorers of creation, which in the beginning reflected their original light purely, started to distort the purity of the reflection in their mirrors/minds because of the emotional experiences or negative feelings that they observed in their voyages. These began to present themselves as distortions or shadows of the images reflected in their mirrors/minds. To clarify, I'll refer to another idea from my book, *Spirituality 103*, where I explain that the clarity of your reflection in the mirror depends on the purity of your vision. As each man's mind discovers Creation, it will reflect many discrepant visions of the same experiences in their mirrors. These variants depend on individual experiences and the exchanging of knowledge. These differences bring discrepancies between travelers over who is right, which hampers the real understanding of these experiences.

The quote uses the distorted images in the mirrors of fun houses as a comparison to what happens when we see each other in our human interactions, where our experiences, dimmed by emotions, prevent us from seeing how we really are in our mirror or in different mirrors. In my book, I emphasize that the only way to see who we really are is recognizing that there are distortions or shadows in our mirror, and in other mirrors, and that we must learn how to clean the distortion of our mirrors with the

"Windex" of forgiveness. After all, we are responsible for its alteration.

To have a pure vision of our reflection (correct self-esteem) and understand that we really are sons of light, we cannot depend on the reflection in other people's mirrors, even if they are our most loved ones. Only looking at ourselves with the eyes of the Spirit in its Magical Mirror, we will see ourselves in our pure light.

Human personalities are composed of programs inherited in the DNA of their ancestors; what has been learned throughout life experiences, which includes the parents' influence; scholarly and religious education; and independent reading of books. The parents' influences, positive or negative, usually are the most entrenched in their characteristics. All these influences, being conscious or subconscious recordings, could hypothetically be reprogrammed if the person makes use of a profound introspection of their life with the support of adequate therapists and loved ones.

Even though we can make use of the perceptions of others regarding our personality and of the "normal" guides in psychology books, we must remember that what they see in our mirror also has a level of distortion, and we cannot use these solely as sources for reprogramming. Yes, we can normalize our actions within the parameters established by our relationships and therapists, but our primary source of transformation is the one that originates in and reflects from our Magical Mirror (mind), after using forgiveness to understand and clean all the shadows falsely created by our emotional experiences.

## EXERCISES TO INTERNALIZE THE MESSAGE

Begin with the Meditation of the Colorful Bath of Love. (See References and Resources.)

Make a list of your good and bad personality traits (you can consult loved ones). Observe if any of these traits come from your parents, and if not, consider where you copied them from. Note how some only present themselves during stressful or difficult situations. They usually manifest from past periods of your life and wouldn't appear in normal states. The characteristics that we strive for must be based on the Golden Rule, where our actions must be consonant with not doing to others what we don't like done to ourselves. This rule is born from empathy with our brotherhood as sons of God, where these biblical phrases apply: "Thou shalt love the Lord thy God with all thy heart, and with all thy soul, and with all thy mind. Thou shalt love thy neighbor as thyself" (Matthew 22:34-40). And this other one, "Truly I tell you, whatever you did for one of the least of these brothers and sisters of mine, you did for me" (Matthew 25: 40-46).

Many of the negative characteristics stay programmed in the subconscious during the stages of youth. They are misunderstood lessons of love that were archived as failures, guilt, or embarrassment because of unreal expectations of perfection imposed by others or ourselves. These are the ones that in my book, *Spirituality 103*, are healed with the key of forgiveness, understanding the mistakes of mental development, or lessons of love. We must remember that the primordial creative mind (Magical Mirror) does not judge or punish us because our free will, with patience and infinite compassion, allows us to learn from our mistakes.

Review your lives; think about the time of the most stressful events and observe how now, they don't seem as catastrophic as they appeared in the past. Don't pass judgment on your failures, but be proud of the learning experiences that allowed you to be a better human being. Understand that the programs received by your parents are the ones they received from their own parents and that they couldn't break the chain of programming even though they didn't like it. Converse with your parents about this, and discard the patterns that make you and others unhappy based on the Golden Rule.

# QUOTE 4

*We must remember every difficult or painful experience as a lesson of love.*

Forgiveness can only come from realizing that every action that ends in failure or suffering is not a punishment, but a lesson of love that teaches us not to repeat it. I tell my patients, "The wisest men are the ones who have made the most mistakes." To understand what a lesson of love is, I tell them the following tale.

One day, while a mother was doing the dishes, she observed her three-year-old child getting close to the gas stove where there was a pot filled with rice, and he tried to reach for the fire. The mother quickly ran to the child and slapped his little hand, yelling, "No, no, that's bad!" The boy's reaction was to cry, for he could not understand his punishment.

Eight years later, while taking care of his three-year-old brother while his mom used the bathroom, he sees that his little brother comes too close to the gas stove and tries to do the same thing; he slaps his little hand and removes him from the danger. In that instant, the child understands the lesson of love that his mother had taught him in the past. In the same way, God exposes us to awkward situations where we start to become more conscious as we go through many lessons of love that rectify our diversions from the path, and it's not until time goes by that we begin to understand them.

Free will allows us to learn by choosing between multiple options that have many variable results. All those experiences, be they good or bad, accumulate as wisdom that we will use in future decisions. All experiences come with a lesson of love.

## EXERCISES TO INTERNALIZE THE MESSAGE

Begin with the Meditation of the Colorful Bath of Love. (See References and Resources.)

Review all the lessons of love that life offered you and look for what you learned that applies to your present life. Ask yourself: did I have the necessary maturity and understanding to comprehend this event? Rarely, in the past, we had the maturity to understand the event as a lesson of love. Don't be ashamed for not having the capacity to process the experience, for you didn't know what you were doing.

Practice the key to forgiveness discussed in my book *Spirituality 103,* in order to liberate guilt associated with our past mistakes (see the copy in the study materials).

# QUOTE 5

*If you don't learn to listen to the music of the spirit, you will never dance to your life's melody in rhythm.*

The whole universe is a loving musical score. If we don't tune our spirit's ears by learning our lessons of love and instead use our human ears, we are likely to hear only out-of-tune melodies coming from the material universe. These melodies muffle the harmonious music inside the deepest recesses of our spirit.

When we learn to dampen the loud noise coming from instruments that get out of tune because of our ego's emotions, our whole organism vibrates in consonance with the Melodious Silence of the Cosmos. Only then can we say that we have our own inner music and will never lose the rhythm of our life's dance!

## EXERCISES TO INTERNALIZE THE MESSAGE.

Begin with the Meditation of the Colorful Bath of Love. (See References and Resources.)

Within the silence of our material mind, which stops the continuous chatter of the ego, we will start to develop our spirit's musical ear. That, together with vegan nutrition and a mental detox from the guilt created by negative emotions, is the best way to awaken our spirit's musical ear to hear the spirit's music better.

# QUOTE 6

*The solution to the paradigm of suffering is that Creation is a perfect imperfection; an organized disorder; an immeasurable time; and a constant quest for balance, where the light is just shades of shadow, and the shadows are shades of light.*

To understand the essential message of this quote, we must understand what I discuss in my books as the fundamental origin of suffering: attachment. The definition of attachment, as defined in the book *Spirituality 103: The Forgiveness Code*, reads as follows: "Attachment: the need or emotional addiction of repeating pleasant physical or mental experiences." In its most immature form, it can be the worst addiction a human being can experience, and it is the primary source of suffering. It can be an appropriate sensation in some cases and inappropriate in others. During the exploratory process of creation, the children of men saw only distortions of what they observed in their minds (mirrors), corrupted by their previous experiences. These experiences were classified as good or bad, and travelers chose their favorite places and avoided the unpleasant ones. If they were assigned their preferred areas in their exploratory assignments, they were pleased, but if they were assigned the less favored ones, they felt very annoyed and frustrated. We must note that the concordance of the favorite ones was very subjective and variable in each case.

As expressed in the quote, creation is a process of seeking the appropriate balance between the extreme poles of a continuously changing phenomenon. There is no perfect goal, but rather a process of continuous perfecting of an experience that is more inclusive than the one before. The new goal motivates us to get better results, even if we don't reach perfection. The quote stresses the continuously changing nature of all manifestations of Creation and all the interpretations of the observations in the explorer's minds. The Magical Mirror doesn't see any expression of its creation as better than another because each one carries a lesson of love specific to the explorer's individual capabilities. This comes from another concept from my book, *Spirituality 103*, "When the Warrior learns to see the universe through the reflection of the Magical Mirror, he only sees the light or love."

## EXERCISES TO INTERNALIZE THE MESSAGE

Begin with the Meditation of the Colorful Bath of Love. (See References and Resources.)

We must carefully revise the events that made us happy throughout different stages of our lives. Observe the origin of this happiness and notice if it comes from your own successes or from the achievements of others in your family or relationships. What motivated its search? Was it your satisfaction, or the desire to please others?

Do you prefer postponing your goals so that others can continuously obtain theirs? This tendency is seen frequently in mothers, wives with children, and husbands, respectively. Observe if the acquired happiness was permanent or transitory. Do you remember situations where obtaining your goal made you feel disappointed? If your actions were influenced by wanting to increase your income, or earn more authority and respect, did the results satisfy your expectations? As a counterpoint, due to familiar or individual reasons, which pleasant experience or thing did you have to abandon?

Real sadness comes from the emptiness created when we forget our common origin from the fountain of light and love, the Magical Mirror, a space that will never be fulfilled by any mundane event or recognition. Only by following the requests of our heart, we can open our eyes and feel happy and motivated to confront the lessons of love that each new day brings. No treasure or material power in this world will guarantee us health, life, or eternal youth. Let’s always learn to find the light in our shadows.

# QUOTE 7

*In the Magical Mirror of your mind, the clarity of your reflection (self-esteem) depends on the purity of your vision.*

Let's begin by remembering that every area and experience inside Creation has its place and purpose, even if we don't agree with it. Also, let's remember that all distortions of our image are emotional mirages of our primordial image created in the Magical Mirror. After we learn that we don't have to be perfect and that we're only looking to improve ourselves, and that this objective is only obtained by making mistakes, we can stop blaming ourselves or letting others censure us for these valuable learning experiences. In your next business or academic meeting, dare to demand, "He who has never made a mistake, raise your hand." I still haven't found anyone who never made a mistake!

If we insist on using prescription lenses fogged by the guilt for our mistakes, we will never see the beauty of our image reflected in our mirrors. That's why we must learn to clean our lenses with the "Windex" of forgiveness. By learning to be tolerant and compassionate with our lessons of love, we become tolerant and compassionate with other travelers along our path. This process brings us to trust that we were created with all the appropriate tools to carry out our exploratory mission, and finally, to recognize that we're sons of God and Warriors of Light.

## EXERCISES TO INTERNALIZE THE MESSAGE

Begin with the Meditation of the Colorful Bath of Love. (See References and Resources.)

To be able to clear our vision, we must review all the distortions projected by others about ourselves. We should erase them with the exercise of the Key to Forgiveness because they're fictitious. Those who project those distortions don't have the clarity of mind and spirit to appreciate the purity of our image since they don't recognize their own because they ignoring their true nature as sons of light. Maybe this was what Jesus implied in his last words when he said, "Father, forgive them, for they do not know what they are doing" (Luke 23:34). The ignorance of their true essence is what drives humans to act erroneously, which this quote from my books reflects upon: "There are no bad people, only those who have not realized their goodness."

The only way to awaken love in others is to love them, and when you see people that act with fear and distrust, think of them as "unloved" people that have never been loved. These are the "poor in spirit" to whom Jesus wanted to send a message of love with precedence. Let's recognize the source of infinite love that resides inside ourselves and, with them, let's quench the thirst that's still unsatisfied in others.

# QUOTE 8

*Accept that all the knowledge you searched for is already within you.*

True knowledge resides in human experience, but can only be found when you search with the inclusive intention of love and not with the exclusive one of the ego. An inclusive purpose always brings harmonious results, because it includes all the universe's components in its effects. It is the intention to benefit "us" and not just "me," where every decision is made using the Golden Rule, "do unto others as you would have them do unto you" (Matthew 7:12).

This is why free will exposes us to infinite possibilities with unknown results, depending on whether the intentional criteria comes from "us" or from "me." The resulting mistakes and successes will teach us which decisions create the most inclusive results. Since all of Creation is a labor of love from God, all of its effects will be the wisest for each one of his sons. Therefore, each part of Creation carries the wisdom from our maker intrinsically, and that is why I say that the only way to discover it is to look for it inside ourselves. The difficulty lies in that the knowledge is hidden, like a rough diamond inside a lump of coal which needs to be polished by life's experiences (lessons of love).

## EXERCISES TO INTERNALIZE THE MESSAGE

Begin with the Meditation of the Colorful Bath of Love. (See References and Resources.)

Creativity is one of the qualities God implanted in us, but its activation only occurs when there is an effort to discover it within the vast matrix of love that sustains us. Most essential discoveries seem to be the result of serendipity without individual cognitive efforts. But those discoverers' minds were already receptive to new ideas because of the accumulated knowledge obtained previously.

The spirit's creative ideas are like seeds in need of fertile soil, a soil (mind) with previous knowledge on how to germinate plants and bring them to fruition. Understand that ideas without a mind to process them are fantasies. Let's try not to look for the meaning of ideas that seem to come out of nowhere. Just write them down and wait for the appropriate moment to put them into practice. I assure you, if you don't, others more in tune with their light will do it. Remember all the times when you discarded a new idea, only to find later that somebody else made it happen? Don't let your fears or those of others stop you from realizing your dreams.

Meditation is a way to activate the creative process in our minds, together with the grasp of scientific and humanistic areas of knowledge. Emotional and physiological detoxification of the organism fertilizes the mind to facilitate the understanding (harvesting) process needed to be able to discover our creativity within the soil of our minds.

# QUOTE 9

*God's most perfect creation in all the universe can be seen in your mirror's reflection.*

The happiness this quote brings to us all is the same joy I felt when my mother told me I was God's most precious gift to her. What I never realized was that she said the same thing to all my siblings, and long after she passed away, I finally understood why she did it. God, like a mother proud of her creation, accepts us as the culmination of its creative effort, since it sees itself reflected in the likeness of the result. For the first time, God sees itself in its Magical Mirror (primordial mind). Mothers, like God, look at us through the eyes of the spirit that can only see the perfect, inner light of the son of God. They do not see the shadows that dwell within the different earthly vessels (sons of men). Therefore, a mother's view of her offspring imitates the purity of God's vision.

On the contrary, the sons of men can only see the variable formats of their biological inheritance. They forgot their divine origins and the spiritual "guest" they carry in their hearts: the son of God. They see the speck in the others' eyes, but not the log in their own. The sons of men that forgot their origin of light will only see the shadows in their brothers, misinterpreting their mistakes as evil acts. This allowed Jesus, the son of God, to say this in front of his captors, "Father, forgive them, for they do not know what they are doing" (Luke 23:34). And I add my version: "Father, forgive them, for they do not recognize they are my siblings and the offspring of my Father." The captors' ignorance about who Jesus really was is what allowed him to see them as blameless, immature children doing shenanigans around the cross. There lies the significance of my quote: "There are no bad people, only those who have not realized their goodness."

## EXERCISES TO INTERNALIZE THE MESSAGE

Begin with the Meditation of the Colorful Bath of Love. (See References and Resources.)

To be able to believe this quote, we should first erase all emotional wounds from our lives because they create the bars of our mental prison and project the shadows that do not allow us to see the perfection of our image. All previous exercises in this book, including the key to forgiveness, the reconnection brought by meditation, and the success in learning from our lessons of love, need to be part of our daily lives. We should remember the many times we have been wrong about the way we see ourselves versus the way others see us, to then accept that God, who is never wrong, can see our perfect image.

# QUOTE 10

*If we only play to win, someone will always end up losing.*

This quote doesn't minimize the seriousness of how we should lead our lives, but rather corrects the vision about what expectations we may have while living. Even though life is not a game, many participate in the experience as if it was a competition with prizes and trophies for the "best" competitors. Shouldn't we ask ourselves if the process of playing could be successful without practicing? In reality, you can't win without practicing or practice without winning, because even though we don't always win while playing, we win by what we learned during practice.

A lot of tournaments last only a few minutes or hours, and someone will always end up winning or losing, whereas the practice sessions that make it possible to compete could mean months of effort that usually nobody recognizes as a benefit for the competitor. Does the second-best fail because he does not get an Olympic medal, even if his record was only a thousandth of a second short? Maybe that is true for the public, press, and sponsors, but the athlete must never feel unsuccessful because it was his best effort. If we only compete with ourselves, someone always ends up winning.

The law of love that governs the universe doesn't pick winners or losers. It only observes—just like the talent parable—how every child of man capitalizes on the talents he was provided and how he used them to help others develop their skills. All of these efforts to win the game of love uncover the hidden wisdom already contained within the athlete's heart. That wisdom allows him to erase the shadows off his image and the image of others that compete with him. That's why all sons of man who give their maximum effort are always awarded in the game of life with the wisdom (gold medal) they discover in their hearts.

## EXERCISES TO INTERNALIZE THE MESSAGE

Begin with the Meditation of the Colorful Bath of Love. (See References and Resources.)

Let's pray and meditate on the previous words and review what we learned in all the practices for our competitions. Let's find all the medals of knowledge we got for our efforts. Those recognized by the audience as winners have not always obtained or applied the same knowledge we gained through our "failures." Therefore, when we remember our classmates in different school levels, we can observe how those who were more successful in their careers and profession were not always the ones with the best qualifications or prizes. Remember that in the game of life, we all win if we put our best effort forward.

# QUOTE 11

*Material DNA (biological) and anti-material DNA (spiritual) are like two historical scripts that embrace the dance of Shiva, with creative and destructive rhythms like yin and yang to ensure a harmonious universal dance.*

This poetic quote encompasses the secret of Creation, of its cycles, and of its history. The human genome and the genome of other organisms have two lines of genes woven together in a beautiful spiral where they seem to hug each other in a rhythmic dance that follows the music of creation. This spiral represents the nature of the two universal cycles, the gradual contrast of the yin and yang that belongs to the oriental vision of the human experience. The nature of the universal cycles is evident in the cycles of day and night, climatic seasons, menstrual cycles in females, stages of life and death, physiological cycles of the human organism, the transmission of sound and light waves, et cetera.

All experiences have a beginning and an end, but in this cyclic universe, the end is always the beginning of another cycle, just like the day goes to sleep in its night and the night wakes up to the beginning of a new day. Science knows that the universe, even though it seems to be expanding continuously, will come to the end of its expansion cycle (yang) and will initiate its new period of contraction (yin) until its resting point from its origin in the transitory dream of its black hole.

The history of this path and its cycles are archived in the book of life or Akashic registry. If we revise the nature of man by following my book *Spirituality 101*, humans were created in two manifestations: a transitory biological human being that is born and dies, or the son of man; and a spiritual immortal, or the son of God. They both coexist intertwined like DNA. Their history or memories of the journey are first archived in the biological DNA, which tries to improve the short, biological evolutionary experience cycle by learning and selecting the best transformational qualities of the organism. Darwin called this natural selection. The second stage is the archiving of all learned experiences by the son of God (spirit-soul) throughout his journey as the son of man. This last history is full of the wisdom accumulated from the successes and mistakes the son of man experiences thanks to his free will. For more details about this process, please refer to *Spirituality 103.*

## EXERCISES TO INTERNALIZE THE MESSAGE

Begin with the Meditation of the Colorful Bath of Love. (See References and Resources.)

Review the previous information about the Middle Road and integrate it to the universal cycles. Observe how these global cycles manifest incessantly in your lives, and how no manifestation has a beginning or an ending. Meditate often, because understanding this lesson is done with the heart, not the brain.

# QUOTE 12

*In our multidimensional mental journey, there are no incorrect trails, only necessary detours to complete pending destinations and finalize our universal experience.*

To understand this quote, we must review our previous discussion about suffering where we affirm that all good or bad experiences are lessons of love. Remember that it's the lack of awareness that makes these experiences seem unpleasant and unfair in our eyes. When revising our lives, many of us tend to understand these negative experiences as wastes of our time which we regret, and we think that if we had chosen differently, our lives would be better.

To refute this interpretation, I offer my patients a trip to their past in a time machine so that they have the option to change their decisions. But when I help them to imagine traveling back in a time machine to those exact past moments, they all repeat the same choices. The main reason for this phenomenon is that when we get on the time machine and begin our trip to the past, all of our experiences—good and bad—are entirely erased after the point we are traveling to, and we go back to the same dilemma from the same perspective we had back then.

To help understand how the soul processes the assignment to choose its body, I came up with this fictitious story. Before the soul chooses its earthly guest, it enters a spiritual contract with its guardian angel about what decision will help it to grow more spiritually. After understanding the experience that awaits, the soul signs the agreement on its way down because it understands that it's the best option. That's why we can't regret any of our past experiences, because they're all lessons of love that we must accept as necessary to our spiritual growth.

Remember always that all the apparent detours of our preferred routes are necessary to be able to arrive at our final destination. Bon voyage!

## EXERCISES TO INTERNALIZE THE MESSAGE

Begin with the Meditation of the Colorful Bath of Love. (See References and Resources.)

This exercise is one of the most difficult to complete because we must revisit, in detail, all the detours that obstructed our goals in the personal, scholar, familiar, and labor level. Then, we must make use of the code of forgiveness to better understand the lesson of love behind each and every one of them. Let's review every experience and understand there never was a lonely scapegoat, but instead an endless chain of responsibility of many sons of man that didn't know what they were doing.

# QUOTE 13

*When sadness floods your being like a rainstorm, allow the light in your heart to stir up a rainbow of hope and happiness in your life.*

Like in all of the previous quotes, I understand that no manifestation in our lives is out of place or is considered unnecessary for creation. We must remember that all pleasant or unpleasant experiences were influenced by the ones we talked about previously, and that rarely can the sons of man agree on what can make them happy.

Let's review the previous explanations about the Middle Way philosophy again, and how suffering is generated by the attachment to pleasurable experiences and the rejection to unpleasant ones, which are no more than opposing polarities from inevitable universal cycles. Let's review the definition of attachment. Now, let's remember that all loving wisdom is in the pure image created in similarity to the Magical Mirror that represents our spirit, the son of God, and that it's the only source that can satisfy our spiritual void. The terminal emotions that the son of man experiences in his smudged mirror (mind) result in fruitless battles to make pleasurable sensations persist, and to avoid the unpleasant ones.

That's why when emotional storms flood us with the contaminated waters of sadness, we need to look in our sun (heart) for the light that will bring the rainbow of hope and happiness, indicating the end of sorrow.

## EXERCISES TO INTERNALIZE THE MESSAGE

Begin with the Meditation of the Colorful Bath of Love. (See References and Resources.)

Let's review and meditate on each one of the experiences that brought the most sadness into your life. What helped you find the rainbow of hope once again? Let's apply what we've learned about lessons of love and the key to forgiveness, and erase all traces of guilt from the dictionary of love. Let's make an empathic connection with other beings in similar situations, and maybe visit groups that provide support in similar cases. Let's learn to express our emotions without turning into victims of others' actions, remembering that all situations in our lives have a place inside the group of lessons of love that will help us polish the distortions in our mirrors.

# QUOTE 14

*God's name is so immense, it does not fit in my mouth.*

This quote, from my book *Spirituality 101*, tries to universalize the sectarian message of some religions that promote proselytism and separation between God's children. We must ask ourselves, if all Judeo-Christian and Muslim beliefs have a common origin in Adam's lineage, why have they been experiencing so much conflict with the same God as its origin?

The quote is born from the written teachings of the Old Testament, wherein Hebrew tradition affirms that God was named in many different ways in the Bible. All the names were allowed to be pronounced by man because they represented the earthly qualities of his divinity, but they all originated from the root of his real name, the acrostic YHWH. These syllables could only be written, but not pronounced, because saying them out loud was a sin. It means "I am what I am," which is what the burning bush answered to Moses when he asked who he was. All names for God refer to a sacred symbol. To avoid committing a sin, the Hebrews referred to that symbol as, "He whose name is so big, it does not fit in my mouth."

From that tradition, I can deduct why men understood and interpreted God in so many ways. We, sons of the great Magic Mirror, made in its image and likeness, are part of the vastness of his wisdom. Our mundane, material mirror (mind), with its distortions of its human reflection, can't understand more than a subjective, minimal part of the vastness of God. That's why, in his human limitation, when man pronounced the holy name, it could only grasp but a tiny portion of what God is, adjusted to its capabilities. This resulted in as many versions of God, as there were many men who wanted to know him.

As a result, there are many valid but limited versions of the same God, giving origin to all sectarian discrepancies that exist today. It seems that man was making God fit his image and likeness, and not accepting to be an image and likeness of God! That's why we must have tolerance with our discrepant visions of God, because they all have part of the truth, but none have the absolute truth.

Our way of understanding God doesn't matter if we can live in the harmony of the

Golden Rule with our brothers. Perhaps then, we will understand the meaning of this quote: "All roads lead to heaven but not at the same time." Let's allow our lineage to be recognized, thanks to our actions as sons of God.

## EXERCISES TO INTERNALIZE THE MESSAGE

Begin with the Meditation of the Colorful Bath of Love. (See References and Resources.)

When we are gathered with believers of diverse religions, we should listen to their version of God and not impose ours, since this will enrich the interpretations of both. In my journey through the studies of many non-Christian religions, I found new ways of studying parts of the Bible that I couldn't understand before. Like the previous meditation, imagine the tremendous creative energy of love as a fountain of white light in the center of the universe. As it expands throughout Creation, it divides into infinite tonalities of colors that adjust to the need of all of Creation's sons to feel loved. See how those rays fill every corner of our universe, and then maybe you'll understand that "God's name is so immense, it does not fit in our mouths."

# QUOTE 15

*We are like rivers that always flow to God's great ocean of love.*

This quote is based on the holographic concept of creation that is implied in the biblical phrase, "Whatever you did for one of the least of these brothers and sisters of mine, you did for me" (Mathew 25:40). Let's take a look at the definition of the word hologram. Hologram: a three-dimensional projection obtained from a flat image by laser-ray techniques, where the original can be replicated by any of its parts. This suggests that the information of the entire image is stored in each of its parts, and that there is an intrinsic form of communication among all of them which does not depend on space and time.

In simple words, there's not a place in all of Creation where God isn't present. This biblical quote reinforces this concept: "For where two or three gather in my name, there am I with them" (Matthew 18:20).

Here's another way to see the meaning of this quote.

The universe is like a great ocean of love, and we are all like rivers that flow toward it. In any given moment, we may believe that we are just individual rivers, but by uniting with the great ocean, we realize that we were never really separated from it. Some of us emerge as large and turbulent rivers, others as peaceful or weak streams, but we are never alone in our path. What affects the ocean, in turn, affects the river, and what affects the river has repercussions on the ocean. Likewise, heaven's love relationship with earth's love manifests in an inexorable continuity. That's why, in the hands of a wise person, a glance with the appropriate intention can balance the universe.

## EXERCISES TO INTERNALIZE THE MESSAGE

Begin with the Meditation of the Colorful Bath of Love. (See References and Resources.)

Let's try to really understand that very fundamental nature that we mentioned in the poem by observing the presence of love in every daily act. Visualize that you are like rivers that flow from the vast ocean of love, and that all images that come through our eyes are a creation of love. Put your feet on the ground, and in its firmness feel how the love of God supports you. When you inhale, feel how love comes in and expands through your lungs. When you ingest and chew food and liquids, explore how you can savor the love in your meal and how swallowing vitalizes you. When you shower, feel how the water baptizes and purifies you with love and when you give in to sleep, feel how you dissolve once again into the ocean of love from where you originated.

# QUOTE 16

*Wise is the one that lives with his feet on the ground, but his eyes on heaven.*

This sentence summarizes the purpose of universal Creation's infinite and majestic exploratory trip, assigned to each one of God's children. We can imagine the initial phase of Creation as an immense treasure hidden in the shadows of the light's infinite hues, where only with varied experiences can God's children discover the map that will then guide them on their way back.

It's in this Creation where up and down, in and out, light and shadow, feminine and masculine, matter and antimatter, and the son of God and the son of man intertwine like the two chains of our DNA in the harmonious continuity of the wisdom of love. This wisdom comes from all the shades of color in the universe that we can choose to experience, thanks to our free will.

The book titled *Spirituality 103* refers to this relationship as the alchemical matrimony between light and its shadow, where all great wise men (teachers) who learn how to look with the eyes of the spirit and to walk through all creation with their feet on the ground, but their eyes on heaven, are born. That was Jesus' example when he demonstrated to men that they could amalgamate the son of God with the son of man and the wisdom of Christ. Let's never lose the hope of finding the infinite light that is hidden within our hearts, under the shadows of our human emotions.

## EXERCISES TO INTERNALIZE THE MESSAGE

Begin with the Meditation of the Colorful Bath of Love. (See References and Resources.)

Let's reclassify our shadow's experiences as necessary and just based on the capacity we had at the moment of creating them, and let's find in them the light that is born from the lessons of love that we needed to learn. Let's use meditation, the key to forgiveness, and patience to obtain the wisdom hidden in our shadows.

Let's learn to develop patience with ourselves and others who are in the process of learning from their mistakes, because God and others have had patience with us. Remember that the wisest men have also been the ones to make the most mistakes. The road to wisdom is one in which our steps sometimes alternate between going forward and going backward, but when we finish the trip, the final result has always taken us forward. Never lose the hope of completing your mission.

# QUOTE 17

*The ego kidnaps the happiness in our hearts.*

Even if the ego has been rightfully designated as the leading cause for our grievances, we must review in my books that we create the ego with our feelings of loneliness, fear, and anger when we separate ourselves from our primary source of light at the beginning of our exploratory journey throughout creation. The son of man, or shadow warrior, appears when the son of God starts to stray away from his origin and discovers the hidden shadows of his own light. This is how it begins to disconnect and forget its divine origin. The resulting sensation of loneliness and abandonment wraps him in the sadness born of the emotional shadows that fog its vision in the mirror of its mind.

This is where the son of man, now shadow warrior, creates a false god to appease its loneliness. That false god looks like the shadow warrior, and confronts the true God with an infinite source of shadows for the sons of men. This humanized God makes the sons of God forget their common spiritual lineage and only remember their physical heritage as sons of other men.

When trapped in the limited perspective of the three-dimensional material world for the first time, man can experience birth, get older, get sick, and die. This reality makes him a slave to the fears of death and of wasting precious time in his material life. Then, he falls prisoner to the ego's individualism, and this creates the lifestyle that will define the rest of his life—selfishness. The universe in which the ego places us is like a mental jail created by the bars of emotions that, by their own changing nature, will never be able to offer us permanent happiness. Individualism and loss of touch with our common origin turn our lives into a nightmare full of suffering, intertwined with a few moments of joy.

The ego, covering the light in our hearts with its shadow, steals the happiness from our being and takes us to battle against other light warriors who can't also recognize the light in their shadows. That's why shadow warriors can never be happy.

## EXERCISES TO INTERNALIZE THE MESSAGE

Begin with the Meditation of the Colorful Bath of Love. (See References and Resources.)

This phrase that was in the entrance of the school of mysteries in Delphi must govern our ego studies: "Before knowing God, know yourself." Because the ego is programming distorted by emotions, we must know in detail the obsolete and selfish programming that composes it, and little by little we can reprogram it with some based in the wisdom of love. These new programs surge from the experiences learned from the lessons of love that we will find in our shadows.

Remember that every new light discovered in our shadows reminds us that just as with the prodigal son, they guide us on our way back to our Father's house.

# QUOTE 18

*Those with a blind spirit*
*can never find love.*

First, let us remember the phrase, "When a man learns to look through the eyes of the spirit, he can only see love." We must understand that humans were created with a dual nature, first as sons of God and then as God's vehicle to experience its creation, the son of man. I explained this duality extensively in my first book, *Spirituality 101*, where the son of man is not conscious of his spiritual nature as the son of God, thanks to the emotional interference of his ego. This is why he lives alienated from the essential part of his being, his soul or spirit. These are the people who get their happiness stolen by their egos. The ego also tricks them by distorting the light from the son of God (warrior of light) with the shadows of their own emotions.

Those who disconnect their inner light, or son of God, cannot remember who they are, where they came from, or where they are going. They live experiencing emotional attachments to earthly life, and fear old age, sickness, and death, with no hope of returning to their place of origin, their Father's house. They cannot understand love because they have never felt loved, and they cannot understand compassion because they cannot understand forgiveness. They do not appreciate patience because they believe they are running out of time to reach the mundane successes their selfish ambition seeks.

These are the people who mistake free will for permission to live a life in which they are not responsible for the consequences of their actions on others who share our universe. Instead, they unload their responsibilities by blaming their failures on others. When others are successful where they have failed, they get jealous and angry, and dive into the depths of a lonely hell created by their shadows. Nothing fulfills their spiritual void, created by their disconnect from their inner light. There are no titles, degrees, bank accounts, or plastic surgeries that can bring back their happiness or youth. These are the blind of spirit, who can never find love because they cannot recognize their soul.

These are the ones Jesus spoke to, looking into their eyes, when he said, "Father, forgive them, for they do not know what they are doing" (Lucas 23:34). The wisdom, patience, and compassion of that vision ensured the suffering created by the actions of the blind of spirit would result in different lessons of love to help them remember their spiritual inheritance as sons of God. These results can be obtained with the key to forgiveness, which allows the son of man to learn from his mistakes when he accepts his responsibility and understand the negative consequences of his actions.

## EXERCISES TO INTERNALIZE THE MESSAGE

Begin with the Meditation of the Colorful Bath of Love. (See References and Resources.)

Let us do an introspection about what we are looking for to be happy. What are those goals? Where did they come from? Are they our heart's desires, or were they placed there by others or by social pressures? Have those who reached some of their goals achieved real happiness? The goals we have achieved, have they filled us with permanent joy or have they been fleeting? Do you share your wishes with your loved ones?

How do you feel when you fail, and who do you make responsible for your failure? How do you feel when others who share their lives with you reach goals you couldn't? Review your attitude towards death, and how you would confront it if it was near. Is your whole family satisfied and happy with how you provide for their well-being? When one of your loved ones fails in the pursuit of a goal, how do you support them? Do you feel loved by your family, colleagues, or yourself? Do you take medication for anxiety, sadness, or sleep? Are you delighted with your life?

Learn to listen to the voice of your spirit when you face suffering or failure, so that little by little you remember who you are, where you came from, and where you are going. Do not become blind of spirit, roaming the streets of life, begging for scraps of love from others.

# QUOTE 19

*Codependents: those who are spiritually disabled and use others as crutches to walk through life.*

Codependency is the type of love that kills us. It asphyxiates us with its hugs, and it deprives us of the oxygen for our souls. These are the loved ones that think they know what will give us happiness better than us. They are the same spiritually blind ones that cannot find the inner strength of their light and are like parasites or cancer that can only subsist by stealing the light of others. They make themselves essential in our lives, taking the free will given to us by the creative mind of the universe, which allows us to learn through trial and error.

Based on their mistakes and fears, many of these people accidentally project this attitude that will never allow them to develop their potential. In their insecurity, they feel that they can obtain their successes through other people's actions, taking credit for them. In psychology, this is a dysfunctional relationship between two people who are united by a link in which the strongest part imposes its will upon the weaker part. This alliance is similar that of a disabled person, where the disabled person can't walk without their cane, and the cane is useless without the disabled person.

This relationship is like our relationship with our ego, in which our ego debilitates us by creating emotional conflicts among the sons of men, so that we may never find the light or remember the way back to our

Father's house. The dominant figure in the codependent relationship forces their intentions by diminishing the dependent figure's self-confidence when resolving the life experiences that free will provides. It's similar to a parasite's relationship with its host, or to that of a cancer cell with a normal cell. Cancer can't produce its own energy, and those malignant cells die without the normal cell's presence. Every dominant being in a codependent relationship is like cancer to the dependent part, and because it's hungry for love that it can't find within itself, it steals it from others in their life.

These relationships often happen in couples and mother-father relations, and they are the origin of the suffering that, many times, takes our brothers to a state of addiction with alcoholism, drug abuse, psychiatric imbalances, economic exploitation, gender, and racial injustice.

## EXERCISES TO INTERNALIZE THE MESSAGE

Begin with the Meditation of the Colorful Bath of Love. (See References and Resources.)

Let's review our lives and see how codependent relationships have marked our life's road and suffering. Let's recognize what role we've taken in each of our relationships. Observe how many of these codependent relationships we learned from our parents or caretakers and how, on many occasions, we've passed them on to our children. Let's begin applying the key to forgiveness to all of those who imposed those relations on us, and then with ourselves for having imposed them on others. We must remember that on many occasions, it was our own emotions and ignorance that led us to promote this type of relationship. Let's remember Jesus' final phrase on the cross, "Father, forgive them, for they don't know what they're doing" (Luke 23:24). Let's talk to our children, let's own up to our mistakes, and let's support them in breaking the codependent chains linked to those in our lives who are spiritually disabled.

# QUOTE 20

*Authentic spiritual beings think, talk, and act in harmony with love, compassion, and patience.*

Human beings must recognize the original brand of their vehicle (body), versus the imitation that life is trying to pass off as the real thing, in order to lead an authentic life. Our authenticity is based on the exclusive seal of love and light of our celestial factory, that made us entirely to its image and likeness.

The sons of man, full of fear after leaving the security of Eden's garden, feel restrained by the loneliness created by the terror of disconnecting with their light source. They then start to believe that they're only a knockoff of God's son, who doesn't have an eternal warranty and only has the guarantee of life on Earth. I propose a metaphor: a human being who is repaired like a car in a body shop that lacks original parts, and is molded with the decorative Bondo (filler) of the ego's emotions, gets dented, and deforms quickly due to crashes with other vehicles in the highway of life. This creates suffering due to the continuous costs of the repairs that are needed to maintain fictitious appearances.

The beings that recognize their authentic origin and celestial factory seal are cautious and avoid crashes that would dent their vehicles and others. But when they are struck by other irresponsible drivers, they have a permanent connection with the celestial factory to replace the original pieces and parts for their repair with an eternal warranty. The security of the relationship with their factory warranty allows them to live in congruence, reflecting their light onto others with love, patience, and compassion.

## EXERCISES TO INTERNALIZE THE MESSAGE

Begin with the Meditation of the Colorful Bath of Love. (See References and Resources.)

Living in congruence implies learning to recognize the purity of the treasure that we carry, guarded in our temple's interior. We must maintain the vehicle and drive it in optimum conditions so that the light that activates the motor will serve us eternally until we find our way back to our Father's house. Our way of driving our life's vehicle should be based in respect to the light that resides in all the other vehicles with which we share the highway of life, even if the other drivers haven't recognized the purity of their brand from the celestial factory. With a lot of patience, we can share the source of our pieces with an eternal extended warranty, so that they can recognize little by little that they are also authentic vehicles with the brand of love and light.

# QUOTE 21

*If when you look in the mirror, you only see your shadows, close your eyes, look inside your heart, and you'll always find your light.*

To decipher the meaning of this sentence, let's first revise the previous phrases, "The ego kidnaps our happiness," and "Those blind of spirit never find love."

The common denominators in these two sentences are the loneliness and emptiness that result from our disconnection with our source of creative light that wraps us in the mirage of ego, but like any mirage, it vanishes once we get closer to it, and it will never be able to satisfy our spiritual thirst for living water. The water from the springs of ego, initially structured by the deceitful tastes of emotion, is like intoxicating alcoholic beverages that initially quench our thirst, but quickly make it worse.

The creation of the ego, like the creation of man in Eden, is born from earth (biological material), but we cannot infuse it with the divine breath of the Creator, and it will never have the qualities of the soul. Its heaven is constructed by the bricks of biological matter that is born, grows old, gets sick, and dies, and is set by the unstable plaster of emotions. The creation of ego cannot hold the emotional earthquakes of life because their foundations are built in the sand of the ego and not the rock of the spirit.

The fictitious "paradise" built by the ego is an exclusive world of mine and yours but not ours, where there is no longer any memory of our shared lineage as sons of God, and we only live in continuous contrast in the unending cycle of change that generates time, and the time that creates change.

This way of living with selfishness, and lack of consciousness of our interdependence with the laws of the universe and other beings, turns into a nightmare of suffering with brief moments of happiness.

The shadows created by emotional attachments originate from contrasting the experiences, good and evil, that we experience when we don't perceive what was promised by our ego. This generates fear, frustration, anger, and jealousy, which present themselves in our mirrors as monstrous distortions that destroy our self-love and self-esteem. The search for happiness then focuses on what others affirm will bring us joy, and we stop looking for it in our own hearts, which have been darkened by the fictitious shadows of our emotions. Again, the key to forgiveness is the cleaning agent that will allow us to polish our mirrors until we find, once again, the hidden lights in our shadows. That's why we just should close our eyes and look deep within our hearts to see the light!

## EXERCISES TO INTERNALIZE THE MESSAGE

Begin with the Meditation of the Colorful Bath of Love. (See References and Resources.)

To be able to redirect our gaze into the interior, we must first convince ourselves that the happiness that will fill our spiritual emptiness will not be found in the material kingdom of the ego. We achieve this when we review all the good experiences we've lived and observed in others, and see how none of them continuously satisfies our happiness nor others' happiness permanently. Observe how successful people with fortunes to spend never find happiness, and many of them enter vicious states, get sick, grow old, and die without being able to take anything from this terrestrial experience. Remember your own situations and see how the process of happiness changes and disappears. Observe those who really project happiness, and you'll see how little they have and how much they love themselves and their neighbor. Revise your sacred texts and read them with the eyes of the spirit to see the new light they have saved for you. Meditate and use the key to forgiveness with yourself and others.

# QUOTE 22

*Selfishness fogs up the light in our mirror and the mirrors of others, covering them in the shadows of fear. Be brave and let yourself be loved.*

To understand the importance of this sentence, we must revise the previous one about those "blind in spirit" and remember the term "unloved" from my book, *Spirituality 101*. One of the most challenging processes is allowing others to love us with the same carelessness that we allow ourselves to love others. Being loved wakes up the contagious need to love others. That's why in one of my books, I talk about the experience I had when I meditated about what would be written on my tombstone. This is what I saw in my meditation: "Here lies a being that learned to love and be loved." I'm still working on letting people love me!

The unloved are the blind in spirit who will never find love because they live disconnected from the pure love that originates in their spirit. They live immersed in the material privileges of ego, which desensitizes them towards love. Those blind in spirit are totally alienated by the privileges of the material world that trap them in a jail of poverty and deficiency that won't allow them to recognize the love that resides in them.

They live in the shadows of suffering and dislike because they think that no one has ever loved them, and because of that, they haven't learned to love. These are the poor in spirit that Jesus wanted to help so much, and they are the same for which he pleaded, "Father, forgive them, for they don't know what they're doing."

These beings live in the darkest hells of ignorance, and that's where the most grotesque facets of the son of man are born, where their actions coincide almost absolutely with their animal side and almost none with the spiritual origin part. The ignorance of all spiritual qualities turns them into beings insensitive to the pain of others, and they only seek revenge because they don't have what others have. They can only steal the material possessions of others and the love they believe they don't deserve. Love transforms into power and violence among the weakest people because of the law of survival of the fittest. Sex and drugs are used to escape the reality of their suffering. Sociopathy and all other personality disorders are born from these badly loved beings.

These blind in spirit are born from the need to use others for their own selfish purposes.

These unloved people do not trust anyone and never allow others to love them, because they don't understand that someone could. They were never loved in their childhood or upbringing, and they only look for others to respond to their needs due to fear. They are like mistreated domestic animals: we should win their confidence over little by little, first healing their physical and mental illnesses, then mitigating their hunger, and finally offering them a hand that caresses them instead of hitting them. Rehabilitation of a badly loved person takes a lot of patience and compassion because it took them a lot of years to forget their origin from the light. They should be allowed to be loved little by little and learn to see the light in the hearts of others so they can find theirs someday. The ego, with its constant bombardment of negative emotions, ensures that the shadows asphyxiate the little light that the badly loved can perceive. Sadly, this persistent suffering is what makes them rectify their lives after reaching their lowest point. Once they hit rock bottom, the love, compassion, and light from others lead them to be loved and to love others.

## EXERCISES TO INTERNALIZE THE MESSAGE

Begin with the Meditation of the Colorful Bath of Love. (See References and Resources.)

Badly loved beings are complicated to help, and they drain our patience and energy. They often need professional help that includes spiritual fundamentals. We can only bombard them with love and patience because all sons of God have the opportunity to find their light, and we can never lose sight in their healing. For those of us who have the responsibility to care for them, we should never focus on their shadows but instead on their light, so that they can recognize it. Remember, first dissolve your own shadows before trying to help others dissolve theirs (don't carry others' crosses if you can't take your own).

# QUOTE 23

*True love isn't given or taken away: it awakens the love the other person always had.*

This sentence is thoroughly explained in chapter seven of my book, *Spirituality 103*, where love is compared to a piece of coal that contains all the potential love we received during our creation. The lessons of love help us polish our coal roughness (shadow), that doesn't allow our clarity to reflect clearly in our surroundings.

That's why no unloved one can exist because love has always been present within us since creation. The problem is that to be able to polish my diamond in the rough, I must believe that it exists in others and that it can be polished to reflect all its brightness. As explained in my first book, in our universal school we are all in the same universal classroom, in different grades of learning where we alternate between the roles of teacher and student to help each other pass our exams and move on to the next class. We are all grateful to the upperclassmen for all we learned, and we support those that follow us in the lower grades with empathetic compassion.

Similarly, the potential for love that resides in every being or disciple of the school of life can only be discovered and polished by painful experiences, help, and the hope that those who have found their love give us. These are the people we fall in love with when we observe the brilliance in their diamonds, and from whom we learn to polish ours. Love is discovered, never received, given, or taken away. The beings who love only show their love through actions that reflect the brightness of their intentions, and don't need to steal anyone's diamond to feel loved.

Romantic relationships last the time in which both parties can keep learning from one another about how to improve the brightness in their own diamond, but the relationship ends when they don't have anything else to offer each other. That's why, at the end of the relationship, there cannot be any remorse or thinking it was a waste of time because no one can break your heart or steal the love you gave each other. Each one, in its new journey, will retain the love that polished their carbon with the experience from the lessons of love.

## EXERCISES TO INTERNALIZE THE MESSAGE

Begin with the Meditation of the Colorful Bath of Love. (See References and Resources.)

Let's review all loving relationships with family and partners in our life. Let's remember how we fell in love when we saw the brightness in our loved one's diamonds. Let's identify how we lost the capacity to find the light in our partner's heart, but without stopping and seeing ours. Let's add up the events of each relationship in our life. Understand that positive memories shouldn't be affected by negative experiences. Our diamond's brightness can't disappear or be eliminated. It only fogs temporarily, but the fog can be removed by wiping it clean.

Let's understand that it's normal but not necessary to find the brightness in other people's diamonds in order to keep polishing ours. It's never too late to love and be loved again, even if all the new experiences which follow are nothing like the ones before. We should never be afraid of others finding the hidden brightness in our diamonds just because we're scared of remembering the end of a romantic relationship, because we tend to hide our splendor under emotions that disturb its brightness temporarily. To make this fear go away, we must practice the key to forgiveness with each other's separate experiences without assigning unilateral guilt, which allows for better understanding of the shared responsibility of the result.

# QUOTE 24

*Death isn't the end of a story; it's just the beginning of another one.*

To understand this sentence's profound meaning, we must first review how our minds perceive creation as a continuous experience of consciousnesses that travel through the multidimensional universe in vehicles that change to adapt to their new destiny. In each change of vehicle, the ability to archive all perceived experiences is maintained in the constant mental state of our universal memory, the DNA. The communication disconnection that occurs when our conscience descends to more dense plains, in time, limits us from remembering the origin of our trip.

It would seem to some that the end of our traveling experiences is the end of the itinerary, when it's really just a change of vehicle and station towards a new route. This erroneous interpretation comes from the inability to remember previous itineraries, which can be recognized at the end of the assigned course, when we accumulate and learn all the wisdom of our lessons of love. For our limited minds as sons of man, these can seem like lonely trips with a beginning and an end, but before the infinite eyes of our primordial Creator (God), they are inclusive, universal experiences wrongly interpreted by the sons of man by forgetting who they are, where they come from, and what they will go back to.

This implies that every universal experience always was and always will be of

God's creative mind, and that it cannot be assigned a beginning (alpha) or an end (omega), for it includes both. To us, sons of man, our journey's experience can seem like disconnected stories, each with a beginning and an end, but for the Creator's primordial mind, they are like stories intertwined with the script of love in a continuous experience of wisdom without beginning or end.

## EXERCISES TO INTERNALIZE THE MESSAGE

Begin with the Meditation of the Colorful Bath of Love. (See References and Resources.)

To internalize the previous definition, let's make an analogy between our lives and theater plays, where the play represents one of the many universal travel experiences. The characters are our individual learning missions, and the social gathering where the actors meet to evaluate our performance is what happens after "death" or at the end of the play. It doesn't matter how prominent or limited our acting is. What will be evaluated, and what holds relevancy, is how well we did it. Also, when we meet after the performance, those who participated in it with us will not be affected by our fictitious role of villain or hero.

In this get-together, we learn from other actors in order to evaluate how we did on our role or mission, and receive orientation regarding how we can act in new parts that will be assigned to us as we better our performance. As we progress, we will be assigned harder roles and scripts to act out in new plays. In order to be happy in life, we should never think of our parts as good or bad, principal or secondary, for they all have their importance in the play. We must have patience and hope that we can all progress through the significance of our characters.

That is why we must see our deaths as enriching middle acts in the continuity of this experience created by God. Review your lives, and observe if you have been improving your acting in the theater of your life.

# QUOTE 25

*Everything that we need is always available, but not everything that is available is what we need the most.*

The knowledge contained in this simple sentence is immense because within it is the secret to finding happiness. There are many parallels to the sentence, "Even though we all agree that we want to be happy, we rarely agree on how to obtain happiness." Using this paradigm, we choose the quantity and quality of what is offered on the delicious buffet that is our life, where if we don't know how to choose correctly, we could end up with indi-gestion, or an emotional quagmire. Perhaps at our next visit to the buffet, we could try other delights that we had previously passed by. Let's review the concept of happiness that was discussed in the book *Spirituality 101* with a quote from Chapter II.

> *Origins of Suffering*
>
> *The man who does not understand where he comes from and who he really is feels lost in a constant battle with the time and change that he has created with his habits. He also experiences the discrepancy he has with other beings regarding what happiness really is.*
>
> *Living, if we go about it with selfishness and lack of awareness about our interdependence with the universal laws and other beings, turns into a nightmare of suffering from brief moments of happiness (it resembles a soap opera).*

*Happiness is a state of inner balance (well-being) of the mind, which does not depend on what's happening outside of itself.*

*The Son of Man would seem to have forgotten his true origins, by ignorantly creating a fictitious separation from its Creator. Then, to find happiness again, we must:*

*Remember our real roots and understand that the experience of life is just one, where the transcendental manifests in an infinite and changing spectrum of possibilities. The interdependence of one option with another is inevitable, which gives rise to real solidarity with humanity in this experience. We will then realize that the origin of all of this suffering is ignorance of our true original nature.*

These quoted passages reinforce the importance of knowing how to choose what is necessary to facilitate our role and our spiritual and human progress within the confines of the superficial. This progress will pacify the ambitious earthly desires of the ego's loving spiritual intention and eliminate the void created by the disconnection with our Creator. To be able to learn the essential experiences, we must learn to use a holistic, loving intention that seeks "our" happiness and not the egotistical exclusive "my" that only seeks to satisfy the needs of the ego.

We must develop patience and judgment to correctly choose the most inclusive option from those available, which facilitates learning the lessons of love that we need in order to erase the emotional distortion created by the ego's shadows. This knowledge will help us to improve our son-of-man visual acuity and see the loving universe that the spirit will appreciate when it observes us. Nothing that the external material world offers us can satisfy the sadness that our soul feels because its memory of its divine origin has been lost.

Because of this, the most important thing for our happiness appears unavailable in the external reality of our lives, and only the lessons of love can open our eyes to the beauty hidden in our internal knowledge. We learn to recognize what is truly available in the pure light of the reflection of our mirrors and not in the shadows that distort this image and that detour our path back to the house of our Father.

Without this wisdom, our free will becomes a nightmare of suffering with only brief moments of happiness (similar to a soap opera).

## EXERCISES TO INTERNALIZE THE MESSAGE

Begin with the Meditation of the Colorful Bath of Love. (See References and Resources.)

To be able to understand this sentence, we must review each moment in our lives when we were met with a crossroads and see how each intention and act of free will influenced our decisions and resulted in an outcome that didn't live up to our expectations. Remember that the actions that are the most inclusive and might have been the most difficult offer the most gratifying outcomes, especially with long-term goals in mind. The wisest of beings do not chase immediate results or short-term gratification, but rather those that mature slowly in an inclusive and long-lasting experience.

# QUOTE 26

*If we used the same effort it takes to flip through channels on our remote control to turn the pages of a good book, we would tread among infinite paths of knowledge.*

If we recall the books *Spirituality 101* and *Spirituality 1.2,* we can remember that our knowledge is pre-programmed within our biological DNA (heredity) and both consciously and subconsciously by our parents, education, religion, the media, and our socio-geographic influences. This knowledge is not always based on the inclusive wisdom of love, and is indoctrinated frequently by the exclusive nature of the ego. Exclusive knowledge is based on the benefit of the individual, temporary, racial, and socioeconomic guidelines that don't consider the emotional needs of others. This insensitive lifestyle is pure selfishness.

Wisdom based on inclusive knowledge always provides a happy ending for the stories of all individuals, but exclusive knowledge only brings happiness to the included and unhappiness to those excluded from their intention. We live in a world of ego which believes that all experiences in life are disconnected. This leads all that share this belief to experience contrasting cycles of unhappiness and happiness continuously.

This is why the most efficient way to escape from the exclusive lifestyle trap of the ego and its imprisoning emotions is to first review all the programs we have inherited and received during the different stages of our lives. After learning to separate the wheat from the chaff, which we can accomplish by looking for the respective positive and negative effects created in our lives, we can develop our inclusive awareness. This phase is a lifetime process and isn't something that happens overnight. We must let our spirit guide us to learn to filter true nature from information from the media, internet, television, movies, books, social groups, politicians, and religious dogma that in the past we have allowed to program our subconscious minds. This is the message of Jesus, that we can be transformed into new men and women by the inclusive awareness he brought to us with his example.

This new being, guided by the inclusive wisdom of love, will correctly use its mind (the remote control) to tune into the channels and media offering the most inclusive frequencies that transmit the love of the spirit.

## EXERCISES TO INTERNALIZE THE MESSAGE

Begin with the Meditation of the Colorful Bath of Love. (See References and Resources.)

Just like in all the other exercises, the key to forgiveness plays a very important part here, since we must forgive our parents for the exclusive programs we inherited from them, the same way they had to forgive their parents. Afterward, we should forgive ourselves for those that we applied to others and passed on to our children and loved ones. This breaks the endless chain of suffering that we left to our descendants in our DNA, as the Bible refers to in Exodus 20:5:

> *You shall have no other gods before me. You shall not make for yourself an image in the form of anything in heaven above or on the earth beneath or in the waters below. You shall not*

> *bow down to them or worship them; for I, the Lord your God, am a jealous God, punishing the children for the sin of the parents to the third and fourth generation of those who hate me...*

This is why it is our responsibility to help bring forth a new person by transforming the inherited impurities in our DNA, detoxifying both the emotional and the physical experiences recorded there. The emotional aspects we can accomplish with the forgiveness key; the physical we accomplish by detoxifying our bodies through bioethical, nutritional lifestyles and by ingesting plant-based foods free of chemical contaminants.

We will not reach our goals by independently cleansing the mental-spiritual aspect separately from the physical one, without balancing our lives by learning to live with our feet on the ground but our eyes on heaven.

# QUOTE 27

*Enlightenment is just discovering all the beautiful shades of light within our shadows.*

It's easier to understand the message within this sentence if you review the discussion of the Middle Way at the beginning of the book. I always say that beauty is very subjective because, "Beauty is in the eye of the beholder." To understand the apparent ambiguity that takes away power from the observed and shifts it to the observer, we should remember this quote from my books, and its explanation: "When one learns to look at the universe through the eyes of the spirit, you will only see love." If you accept my premise that the primordial mind (Magic Mirror) is the most inclusive intelligence because it can perceive the interdependence of its creation, then intelligence used within an individual perspective must be more limited or exclusive in the understanding of Creation. At first, when the primordial mind observes its results, it feels great satisfaction in its inclusive beauty, and does not see its imperfections or defects in any way, shape, or form.

As the children of God have gone forth reproducing and distancing themselves from their origins in the light, their intelligence has progressively become less inclusive, changing the original perspective observed by the Creator. The book *Spirituality 103* describes the state of progressive separation produced by the children of God during their journey as one full of solitude and sadness, generating the creation of a false god to substitute the one treasured in their memories. This god is the ego, which originates emotions that, in turn, generate shadows that distort and convert the mind's loving initial vision into a self-centered, exclusive one that divides the light artificially into tones of brightness and darkness, beauty and ugliness.

These beings, with their vision distorted by the exclusiveness of its shadows, alienated the initial loving vision of the Spirit with opposing and contrasting views of good and evil. This results in their need to seek good experiences and avoid bad ones continuously. If we review the following quote from *Spirituality 103,* we can better understand the origin of suffering:

> *Our tridimensional universe is the realm of the Warrior of Shadows, where the laws of time and space apply. In this universe, the laws of thermodynamics place the process of matter into a continuous flux of matter to energy, and every physical structure separates into its components due to its entropy. [...] This creates insecurity or fear in the observer, due to the changing or cyclic nature of the universe, augmented by the lack of control in the avoidance all of these changes.*

## EXERCISES TO INTERNALIZE THE MESSAGE

Begin with the Meditation of the Colorful Bath of Love. (See References and Resources.)

We should remember that everything created by this primordial mind had a loving intent, not only in the experiences of the shadows but also in those of the light, even though our exclusive experience or limited understanding sees only a perception of suffering. We must go back and remember that all difficult situations we encounter contain a lesson of love to be discovered. We should revisit our past negative experiences and see how each one of them had a hidden treasure. If we can learn to ask ourselves during each bitter episode, "What is the purpose of this experience?" and not its reason ("Why?"), we will take the initial step to discovering the beautiful shades of the light in our shadows.

Continue practicing the exercise of the key of forgiveness every day to keep reconnecting our mind with the primordial mind, the source of our light.

# QUOTE 28

*The only thing you can see aging in the reflection of my Magic Mirror is the mirror.*

This is a favorite quote to share on my birthdays because within it lies the secret to youth. I share in my books how halfway through my career as a pediatric surgeon, I presented myself as less youthful than my age because of the self-centered attitude projected by my seriousness, self-criticism, and an excessive sense of responsibility that never allowed me to be satisfied and happy with my results. This spiritual immaturity led me to seek perfection in all my actions and goals which, as we have already discussed, is a futile and frustrating exercise. I've been told by friends, family members, and patients that I always seemed to be in a bad mood, always looking for the causes for my apparent failures in those around me then.

My photographs from that period project this image that, compared to how I look today many years later, makes it seem like I have undergone a miraculous rejuvenation. Now not only do I no longer demand perfection as an absolute goal, but instead I am satisfied with making my best efforts in my search for it. I seek to soften my failures with understanding and forgiveness, taking care to only provide my organism with the highest quality ingredients from the plant kingdom, as well as the best quality of spiritual and emotional ingredients from the mental and spiritual kingdom. All this results in the projection of a youthful image that is born from the rejuvenation of each cell by its own love and respect for itself.

This is why each year when I look at the image of my reflection in my mirror, the only thing I see aging is my mirror!

## EXERCISES TO INTERNALIZE THE MESSAGE

Begin with the Meditation of the Colorful Bath of Love. (See References and Resources.)

Here, the use of the key to forgive-
ness directed toward all the frustration and self-criticism that we keep in the deepest depths of our subconscious frees us from the weight and emotional corrosion that ages each cell in our organism. In the same way that the Colorful Bath of Love surrounds us, forgiveness bathes our cells, rejuvenating each one, and beautiful youthfulness emanates and is reflected in our mirror.

# QUOTE 29

*Suffering is only for those who find flaws in their perfection; happiness is for those who find perfection in their flaws.*

We must remember that perfection is an imaginary state of the ego, because what exists in the mind (Magical Mirror) of our Creator is a perfecting process or constant individual evolution that motivates us to discover the hidden treasures in our shadows. People who learn to understand their mistakes as educational lessons of love from the Creator will never find guilty flaws in their universal journey. These people never lose their happiness because they always find something perfect (light) within their flaws (shadows).

They are the blessed who learned to use the key of forgiveness in their lives and never stop learning and discovering new challenges in the perfection of their existence.

## EXERCISES TO INTERNALIZE THE MESSAGE

Begin with the Meditation of the Colorful Bath of Love. (See References and Resources.)

Review your episodes of frustration and anger when you could not get the level of "perfection" imposed by your ego or by people around you. Remember how those "failures" broke your will to continue in your efforts to improve your life, because of the suffering associated with those efforts. Remember the satisfaction of obtaining lesser goals, and don't heed others that minimize those successes with their envy and personal frustrations.

With the key to forgiveness, let us discover the motivation to find new paths, exploring how those apparent failures hid wise lessons of love that prepared us for other opportunities and supported us in perfecting our experience as sons of God and light.

# QUOTE 30

*It doesn't matter what instrument you play in the universal symphony—what's important is that without you, the symphony wouldn't be complete.*

The meaning of this sentence can be clarified if we compare the director of the universal symphonic orchestra with a master watchmaker, and the symphony with a watch he created. In the same way that for the watchmaker, none of the parts that he uses for his creation are more important than others because without any one component, the watch would not keep time, as it is for the musicians in the orchestra that could not play the melody harmoniously.

Equally, the Creator focuses on the holographic interaction of all the parts of his creation and his universal mission and not the individual components of each constituent. It doesn't matter how dominant an instrument is in the universal symphony—what's expected of each musician is its part in the melody. The joy felt by those who listen to the symphony, and those who trust the rhythm of the clock, does not depend on the actions of just one part, but instead in the result of the interaction of them all.

## EXERCISES TO INTERNALIZE THE MESSAGE

Begin with the Meditation of the Colorful Bath of Love. (See References and Resources.)

We should review how we felt in the roles that have been assigned to us in the symphony of life, and how this has influenced our feelings of usefulness and happiness. We can see how feelings of inferiority and envy toward others created unhappiness. To admire and aspire to fill the role that others play can serve as a motivation to improve our participation if it inspires us to keep learning to better our performance without marginalizing others in the symphony.

We can use the key to forgiveness to heal tour dissatisfaction with the role that we play and to forgive the negative feelings generated by envy. We can learn to recognize the importance of our mission within the greater universal context because without our role, the purpose of the Creator would not be complete.

# QUOTE 31

*Nothing is impossible; there are things that are a little bit more improbable and require more patience and effort to be achieved.*

To understand the meaning of this message, we must understand what time and patience are. There are no components from the ego or its exclusive intention here.

Time is a very subjective perception, related to how our minds store the continuity of the different levels of our universal journey in our memory. Even though people have developed tools to measure the continuity of our conscience objectively, the same temporal activity for two different people, when measured precisely, can seem to be totally different. To understand this contradiction, think of how time seems to go on forever when you are bored or suffering, yet seems to fly when you are entertained or enjoying an experience. At the same time, when you are dreaming, your actions happen in a much different temporal perspective.

The relativity of time, as explained by Einstein's theory, follows a now-obsolete concept in which the fastest speed achieved was the speed of light. Current scientific thought now acknowledges that there are particles that supersede the speed of light. In a track and field competition where only three runners compete, the ones in second and third position feel like they are going slower than the runner in the first position, yet when they compare themselves against each other, one is relatively slower or faster. Meanwhile, the one in the first position thinks they are the fastest because there is no one in front. When the goal is reached, the only measure of success is the clocked time it took the first runner to cross the finish line. However, without a measure of time relative to the winner, none of the runners would know how fast they were going, but they would be able to understand the relative order in which they reached the finish line. In theory, there will never be a permanent speed record while there is a possibility of other runners participating in future events.

The fact that there is always the possibility of breaking the previous record shows that there is nothing impossible within the relativity of time. Quantum physics and statistical analysis provide proof. Probabilities grow according to efforts, which can be understood by recognizing that whoever plays the lottery has more chances to win than the one who doesn't get a ticket, and the one who buys more tickets more frequently has more opportunities than the one who plays less. The problem is that relative time is shorter for the son of men because of his or her biologically limited conscience, while the conscience of the son of God surpasses biology and continues throughout all of creation. That is why I say that all requests and actions guided by love will become a reality in God's time, not our time.

We conclude that nothing is impossible, only more improbable, and we only need to increase our efforts and have more patience to allow the seeds that were sowed correctly to bear the desired fruit in the correct season according to God's time.

## EXERCISES TO INTERNALIZE THE MESSAGE

Begin with the Meditation of the Colorful Bath of Love. (See References and Resources.)

Review all your efforts and how successful they were. See if your successes provided the happiness you searched for. Understand that any achievements not motivated by the Golden Rule from the son of God, but by the exclusive motivation of the son of man, will never bear the expected fruit.

At the same time, review how the efforts to attain failed goals that were instead based in the Golden Rule and were inclusive in their loving intentions provided lessons of love that later gave you the tools to achieve other goals successfully. Apply the key to forgiveness to your failures and the successes that did not bring the expected happiness, and use patience to try again.

# QUOTE 32

*There are no incurable illnesses, but some are more difficult to treat than others.*

This message is very similar to the previous one but directed to the therapeutic intention of the therapist and to make the patient's own healing process easier. This sentence will be the topic of one of my next books, and I'll just be focusing on a few fundamental concepts that should be understood now. Let's list some assumptions we must accept and understand about this sentence.

There is no disease without a sick person, meaning that an illness is a very individual and subjective experience. Because of this, we must not treat the illness or symptoms but mainly the sick patient.

Illnesses are a result of our ignorance of how to prevent the imbalances that create the warnings or alarms in our body that we call symptoms, and that we are totally responsible for.

All memory of how these imbalances happen is archived in the memory, or the DNA, of each cell in our bodies.

Anything that enters our body that it does not recognize as beneficial is considered toxic, and the organism will react with immunological responses to protect itself through an inflammatory response.

This inflammatory response will appear, in its early stages, as symptoms that can be corrected initially without much difficulty. However, if the causes of these symptoms are not corrected, the inflammatory process will progress to the more advanced stages of toxicity that we call sicknesses.

Part of the toxic inflammatory process of our ancestors [". . . punishing the children for the sin of the parents to the third and fourth generation . . ." (Exodus 20:5)] makes us more susceptible to certain illnesses than others, depending on the toxicity of our lifestyles.

Most therapists in modern medicine focus on eliminating the symptoms (relieving), but not on eliminating the cause (curing) of the illness. Because of this, the therapists who treat symptoms do not resolve the cause permanently and allow the toxicity to progress to more severe diseases.

The worst toxicity is related to the mental effect of toxic emotions (guilt) stored in the subconscious part of our minds where they subtly inflict the worst illnesses on us. This is where the key to forgiveness achieves the best results.

The most effective healing process is the detoxification of all the accumulated mental and physical toxicity and the reversal of the initial process that produced the intoxication.

To be effective, the process should be guided by the person who caused it and cannot be healed by any other therapeutic process directed by a healer or therapist.

Faith facilitates the process of reconnecting the son of man with the son of God, but true healing will not occur without the effort to learn the lessons of love hidden in the experience of suffering and sickness, and without accepting responsibility for its creation.

The above will help us to stop believing that others are solely responsible, and to avoid creating a feeling of being an innocent victim at the mercy of an unfair destiny. Even hereditary imbalances can be corrected by the new science of epigenetics, which allows us to transform the toxicity inherited in our genome.

When the son of man remembers his origin as the son of God, we will start to see our experiences of suffering as lessons of love. We must understand how to apply the following philosophy: "God offers the most difficult tests to the best students." This converts these students into allies of the light. By understanding and conquering those lessons of love, the student acquires the love that purifies the toxicity (sins) committed by their forebearers.

## EXERCISES TO INTERNALIZE THE MESSAGE

Begin with the Meditation of the Colorful Bath of Love. (See References and Resources.)

Without wasting a single minute, we should eliminate everything toxic from our lifestyle and convert it into something bio-ethical, eliminating all animal and processed products from our diet and all egotistical and exclusive paradigms that prevent us from living in harmony with the Golden Rule. One of the most bioethical diets is the vegan diet and, in my opinion, nutritionally-supported fasts as proposed by Dr. Norman González Chacón, the father of natural medicine in Puerto Rico.

To begin healing the toxicity created by the guilt of pent-up emotions that live in our subconscious mind, we should free them with the exercise of the key to forgiveness.

# QUOTE 33

*All roads lead to heaven . . .*
*but not at the same time.*

To facilitate the understanding of this message, review the explanation of a previous quote, "God's name is so big, it doesn't fit in my mouth." Remember that all human interpretations of God are limited by individuals' experiences throughout their journeys, and by the usual limitations of our human views of the universe without access to the broader vision of the son of God.

All religious beliefs that support our efforts to understand the message of love and solidarity from the son of God can help people according to their historical, geographic, and social environments. They all attempt to make their disciples remember their origin and help them to find the way back home to their father, like the prodigal son, after learning their lessons of love. But each universal traveler of creation progresses at his or her own rhythm since the primordial Creator's mind has infinite patience.

That is why we should avoid imposing our beliefs or our progress in our journey back to heaven (our father's home) onto others at family and social gatherings, and should instead develop patience like our Creator has patience with us.

## EXERCISES TO INTERNALIZE THE MESSAGE

Begin with the Meditation of the Colorful Bath of Love. (See References and Resources.)

Let us review how our beliefs have changed since our childhood, where most of us deviated from the way our parents raised us. Observe how there are many ways to search for the way back home within our family, job, or school environments. Recognize that what unites us in our interpersonal relationships is how we share the universal message of the Golden Rule, even if our practices and devotions are different.

Note which factors brought each person to look for different devotional formats, not because of the individual religious messages, but because of the inappropriate human actions of ecclesiastic representatives and followers of religions. For example, many people like to express their love and respect for God through lively and boisterous external displays, while others prefer using silence and withdrawal to understand God's message better. As sons of men, our concept of God matures gradually, and new ideas require different paradigms to help us understand and live by the Golden Rule.

# QUOTE 34

*Emotions can be instruments of love or weapons of mass destruction, and that is why free will makes us responsible for the consequences of our decisions.*

To understand the powerful effects of emotions, we must first understand how the mind of God made man responsible in the co-creative process of the universe by providing free will. We should try to understand how the experience of life affects our creative process. The science of quantum physics confirms the power of thought of the observer over matter (subatomic particles) in everything manifested in the universe. This confirms the control of mind over matter or the immaterial over the material.

To understand the marvelous creative process of the Primordial Mind or the Magic Mirror, we should accept that all future creative ideas already exist in the consciousness of God, in a potential state with all the tools needed to help them manifest. However, they cannot manifest in the material world without a co-creative force from the mind of the son of man. This is because he molds the inclusive, loving intent of the Spirit in matter. The physical mind becomes the facilitator in a creative process in which God permits the use of free will in finding the pieces of the celestial puzzle and putting them together in loving unity.

This creative process of the son of man becomes a cooperative effort, where the primordial mind lets us become co-creators of its universe and makes us responsible for the results under the law of free will, which teaches us to learn by trial and error. This learning process is directly guided by the type of intent the son of man carries. To facilitate the creative purpose of God, the son of man should be guided by the son of God, who at the same time is governed by the unifying love of all his children and not the self-centered exclusion of the son of man that only cares about himself.

In sum, there are two intentions in the process of co-creation: the inclusive (harmonious) guided by the "we," and the exclusive (egotistical) conducted by the "I" created by the ego of the son of man. Inclusive intentions create experiences of solidarity, love for the co-creator and those around them, and the exclusive tactics that create individual experiences of "me-you" that only bring happiness to some and unhappiness to others. The co-creators who are inclusive are eternal, while the exclusive ones are transitory.

The contrasting experiences can never satisfy the son of man since the temporary satisfaction creates temporary positive emotions when the outcome is agreeable, and negative emotions when the result is disagreeable. Attachment to always expect pleasant experiences makes us suffer when things don't go as expected. Negative emotions like anger and envy intoxicate our souls with the poison we prepare for others when we blame them for our suffering. This is the stress that destroys our lives.

For those weak of spirit that are mentally immature, the damage caused by demeaning words uttered by figures of power such as parents or spouses can be worse than physical blows. These experiences are archived in the mind, leaving behind non-healing wounds that last a lifetime.

## EXERCISES TO INTERNALIZE THE MESSAGE

Begin with the Meditation of the Colorful Bath of Love. (See References and Resources.)

We can look back on how we can dedicate ourselves to search for our own happiness, and remember our happiest and saddest moments. Remember the intentions that guided you. Were they inclusive or exclusive? Out of the best moments, how many were long-lasting? What connections can we see between our emotions and the symptoms in our physical bodies? Observe how others enjoy experiences that don't fulfill you personally. What characteristics can you observe in those whom you admire because they are happy in conditions where you would not be? Are your answers to the previous questions things that are inclusive or exclusive? What have you learned about the exclusive actions you have taken? Use meditation and the key to forgiveness to reconnect with your son of God and learn to be co-creators (facilitators) responsible for inclusive actions that promote the "we" and eliminate exclusive "me-you" thinking.

# QUOTE 35

*"To know is to remember what we have already forgotten"*

*—Plato's Reminiscence Theory*

Plato and Buddha developed this knowledge, and taught that our ignorance of the primordial mind's potential and of the alienation that occurs as a result of the exclusive intentions of the son of men (material mind) are the root of all suffering. All discovery processes in our human experiences are brought about by introspection, and not by external physical explorations while in our earthly journey.

Real knowledge occurs because of the reconnection between the mind of the son of man (material mirror) and the mind of the son of God (Magical Mirror). This reconnection activates a marvelous downloading of ideas and tools to help the earthly manifestation of the son of men. When the son of men's mind disconnects from the son of God's, an emotional whirlwind happens that alternates between states of happiness and adherence to pleasant experiences, and suffering and rejection with the not-so-nice ones. This disconnection makes us falsely feel abandoned by our original light source, bringing forth the ego and the emotions that feed it. Then, the actions that originated from the ego force us to take further exclusive steps that keep us in the confused co-creative cycle of transitory experiences. These experiences are like mirages or imitations of the ones we could have if our intentions were based in love's inclusiveness and the understanding of forgiveness.

The ego takes us to an insatiable path of exclusive ambition that never satisfies its hunger, like this expression says, "Satisfying a hungry man is easy, but satisfying an ambitious one is impossible." The spiritual void created by the disconnection with our source of light cannot be filled by earthly experiences, and the ego's hunger can never be satisfied. Free will, forgiveness, and our Creator's patience allow us to participate in, and make us responsible for, the co-creation of our heaven or hell depending on whether we direct our intentions inclusively or exclusively.

## EXERCISES TO INTERNALIZE THE MESSAGE

Begin with the Meditation of the Colorful Bath of Love. (See References and Resources.)

Let us review all the moments when we had co-creative inclusive or exclusive experiences. Which ones promoted harmony and happiness? Which created different perceptions? Do you remember where the inclusive ideas came from? Which were easier? Which presented more internal or external opposition to acceptance? What or who was their most fervent detractor?

Practice the key to forgiveness in all occasions where you co-create exclusive ideas, since they hide a treasure of lessons of love, which helps you to choose better future actions.

# QUOTE 36

*Love's bright light is hidden like a diamond in the rough, waiting for another loving soul to reveal it with the shine of their own polished diamond.*

This is one of the quotes with the most wisdom, and upon understanding it, the more lenient our negative experiences will be. Its meaning is discussed in detail in the seventh chapter of my book, *Spirituality 103*, which is from where I derive the following discussion. According to the spirit, all of creation is love. Owing to the visual distortion of love that occurs within the material mirror of our mind, children of man can only perceive partial manifestations projected by their emotional states. That is why love can have many variants, including maternal, sexual, or religious, that manifest as needed.

True love can only be found in the potential state of mind of the Creator (Magical Mirror) before exploding in its reflective manifestation, which all its children will discover through loving actions. It is in this same original state that all-inclusive and loving ideas which will later be spread via its children's free will are born. It is my perspective that the love of the Creator is hidden within all minds and all souls of God's children, like an unpolished diamond in a lump of coal. The process of polishing and discovering its brilliance happens when beings learn the lessons of love throughout their journey of discovery in creation. It is the attraction to the splendor of another diamond that is called "falling in love."

Therefore, loving relationships do not create spiritual co-dependencies but mature, responsible interactions. Although the selfish may not like it, no loving relationship is eternal. Everything has a beginning and an end, determined by the capacity of each partner to polish and maintain their diamond's luster. This is why no one can break our hearts (diamonds) or steal their glow, because when the relationship ends, every party carries their own luster intact.

## EXERCISES TO INTERNALIZE THE MESSAGE

Begin with the Meditation of the Colorful Bath of Love. (See References and Resources.)

Revise, in detail, all your loving relationships, from their beginnings until their ends. Recall how you felt during each stage of these, and what caused that feeling. Remember the qualities that initially attracted you, and why you could not see those qualities (brilliance) at the end. Note how negative emotions distorted your capability to see the splendor of your diamond and those of others.

Revise also the times when "your heart was broken" and, seeing how every one of these experiences are lessons of love, use the key to forgiveness to understand the hidden lesson in each encounter without assigning blame. Never lose the hope to love and be loved due to experiences associated with the previous suffering.

# QUOTE 37

*Instead of asking the "why" of difficult experiences, let us find the "what for."*

To understand this quote, we must first review everything previously discussed about the lessons of love hidden in our difficult experiences. The disconnection that occurs between the son of man and the son of God generates a sense of neglect and sadness upon forgetting our spiritual origin and failing to understand our purpose and co-responsibility in the universal creative process we were intended for. This hinders us from viewing the universe with an inclusive look, where every situation has a hidden lesson of love. Our misunderstanding of the experiences may make us question their fairness and their purpose, which may lead us to question the wisdom of the primordial creative mind and the "why" behind its action. This mental attitude can force us to dive into a stormy ocean agitated by negative emotions which will not let us find the lesson of love (life saver) that will save us.

On the contrary, if our connection between the son of man and the son of God is strong, the absence of stifling negative emotions allows us to ask the "what for" out of the experience and find the necessary tools to discover the hidden meaning of love.

## EXERCISES TO INTERNALIZE THE MESSAGE

Begin with the Meditation of the Colorful Bath of Love. (See References and Resources.)

Begin with the key to forgiveness, to free us from all the prisons we lock ourselves in with bars of emotions. Remembering how much we have matured with painful experiences we do not question as unjust, observe how others in worse conditions have emerged victorious. This will help us in our own struggles. Revise how the usage of free will with selfish intentions resulted in negative experiences, which allowed us to rectify our mistakes.

# QUOTE 38

*Our shadows seem larger when we approach the light.*

To understand this enigmatic quote, we should acknowledge the co-responsibility associated with our creation as children of God and men. In my first book, *Spirituality 101*, I suggested that the universal experience is like a school, where the universe is the classroom where all students are together, regardless of their grade level. This school does not have a teacher in charge of the curriculum; instead, all the students share the knowledge learned from the most advanced pupils and those in lower levels in an endless chain of love, patience, and compassion. That is the only curriculum required in life.

This educational format implies that, as the student advances through the levels, they will have more disciples and responsibilities to manage, and their exams will become more complex. The shadows in this quote represent the great responsibility the student confronts each time he or she approaches the brilliant wisdom of the Creator, the light. In this school, it is implicit that students should manifest a significant degree of courage, which will allow them to take the exams of increasing difficulty without fear of failure. The bravery to confront your shadows is born from what is learned from the lessons of love, and from the memories of your spiritual origin of light and love.

## EXERCISES TO INTERNALIZE THE MESSAGE

Begin with the Meditation of the Colorful Bath of Love. (See References and Resources.)

To maintain the courage to keep taking the exams even though we have failed in some of them, we must remember how all failures we experienced before taught us a lesson of love, and that we were never prohibited from retaking the exam. We must feel proud to have passed exams that once seemed insurmountable, and enjoy the happiness that fills us upon seeing how, with our help, other students have learned to pass their exams and their lessons of love.

Always keep your heart and mind open to the continuous process of learning and teaching that encompasses the universal school of life.

# QUOTE 39

*The ground where a man with a compassionate heart treads upon becomes holy land.*

Most of the sons of man live in a world of fantasy created by the ego that, like a dream, would have us believe that we are merely biological beings, which in this fictional universe have a beginning at birth and an ending at death. All religious beliefs teach us that the sacred is separate or external from the body, and that the way to purify oneself is by receiving blessings from the masters or saints that founded the religion or performing pilgrimages to sacred places where they lived.

But is it worth asking how these places or people were purified? The answer is inherent in the teachings they left in their messages. I discussed this in my first book, *Spirituality 101*, where mankind has a dual manifestation as the son of man, living life on the earthly plane, and the son of God, the soul-spirit, who guides the son of man throughout the trials of mundane life. The problem is that the son of man usually lives oblivious to the inexorable accompanying presence of the son of God.

In the Buddhist tradition, the Buddha said, "The answer to life and death is simple, it resides in the palm of my hand."

Jesus said, "The coming of the kingdom of God is not something that can be observed, and nor will people say, 'Here it is,' or 'There it is,' because the kingdom of God is in your midst" (Lucas 17:20-21). My interpretation is that the sacred part of ourselves is the spirit, or soul, given to the son of man at birth to accompany him through the rest of his life.

Therefore, the purification of the son of man is an act of recognizing the sacred element that has always escorted him in life, a state of consciousness always within him. That is why the "sacred" is no more than a mental awareness, where the self acts in an inclusive manner and synchronous with the spoken word, which manifests congruently with his actions. It is a state of harmonious love and compassion that generates happiness in him and all around him. This is a man who lives with his feet on the ground, but his eyes on the heavens.

This is why I say, "The ground where a man with a compassionate heart treads upon becomes holy land."

## EXERCISES TO INTERNALIZE THE MESSAGE

Begin with the Meditation of the Colorful Bath of Love. (See References and Resources.)

Review how you have changed your manner of interacting with others (family, friends, students, religious brethren) as you discovered the son of God in your heart. Take special notes about your qualities of patience and compassion with your mistakes, and those of others. If you have yet to discover the son of God within you, continue practicing the key to forgiveness with all that has happened that you still perceive is a process of suffering and unhappiness.

# QUOTE 40

*The joy of reconnecting cannot occur without disconnection. That is the key to forgiveness.*

In this quote, it is implicit that all processes of knowledge are associated with the free will to learn from our mistakes, and that these errors lead us to experience lessons of love that guide us back to our creative source. The disconnection generates the need to create an imaginary replacement for our magic mirror, which is the ego that thrives off the emotional toxicity of suffering. Yet, paradoxically, it is these experiences of pain that awaken our recollections of the light during these times of solitude. This awakening generates a joyful sensation that fills us with hope and guides us towards the path of love, understanding, and compassion.

This reconnecting is subject to the understanding that suffering is brought on by ignorance of the results of our selfish actions. Those actions were implicitly forgiven under the law of free will that allows us to continue to learn and correct our efforts with these lessons of love and life. I always tell my patients that the wisest men were the ones that erred the most! That is why the key to forgiveness is an infinite fountain of happiness, allowing us to reconnect with our lineage as sons of God. In our pasts, they were the ones that did not know what they had done, and they deserve our forgiveness since we went through the same experiences.

This reconnection is like the one experienced by the prodigal son upon remorsefully returning into the open arms of his loving parent, having remembered the way home.

## EXERCISES TO INTERNALIZE THE MESSAGE

Begin with the Meditation of the Colorful Bath of Love. (See References and Resources.)

There is no way to describe the marvelous sensation when we stop feeling imprisoned by our egos to be perfect, and when we can feel unafraid of failure when we give our best efforts. Our Creator always applauds our efforts as well as our triumphs. The feeling of being loved indiscriminately by our source of light motivates us to continue seeking perfection, without expecting a specific result, and also allows us to have patience and compassion with others on their journey.

The key to forgiveness is the key to reconnect with our Creator, finally.

# QUOTE 41

*A compassionate intention always results in a loving action.*

The meaning of this quote can be inferred from its opposite quote, "A selfish intention always results in a hurtful action." We must then revise, yet again, our notion of free will, which allows us to learn from the natural results of our intentions. Review the difference between inclusive and exclusive actions, as discussed previously. Remember that inclusiveness is how the spirit observes its creation and sees only love ("us"), but in the eyes of its children, the experience is disagreeable or a lesson of love.

Exclusivity sees the universe in divisions separated between what is "yours" and "mine," which are intertwined with attachment and not by love. The bonds of attachment are cemented to certain parts of creation by ego, whereas the bonds of love are flexible and adaptable. When the bonds of attachment are shattered, it is akin to an atomic blast of pain, anger, and suffering, but when the bonds of love break, there are never any radioactive emotions unleashed.

## EXERCISES TO INTERNALIZE THE MESSAGE

Begin with the Meditation of the Colorful Bath of Love. (See References and Resources.)

To avoid repeating many painful lessons of love, we should have more inclusive intentions and less exclusive ones. Revise how, in different stages and experiences of life, having intentions of one sort or another led us to lessons or experiences of love. Use the key to forgiveness to implement what was learned from lessons of love created by exclusive intentions, to guide them towards inclusiveness.

# QUOTE 42

*All loving intentions have a happy ending, but that occurs in God's time frame, not yours. That is why you should never expect to get anything back when you make an offering of love.*

Before reading this explanation, review the discussion on time and Einstein's theory of relativity. Remember that the notion of time is very individual, as discussed using the examples of the runners and the distortion of time in dreams. The son of man lives by the rules of time, which is measured by comparing natural cycles like day and night, yearly seasons, or living, aging, and dying. The son of God, who comes from the world of antimatter, exists in a timeless state that cannot be measured via terrestrial guidelines.

Time is a mental state where, as with the runners, our minds are like spaceships where the travelers in the faster ships see time accelerate quicker than those that are slower. The mind of a son of God, like God, is much faster than that of a son of man, where everything is much slower. That is why the quote states that everything occurs first in God's time frame, and not that of man.

Hence why all ideas, actions, and results will not always manifest during our expected timelines. We should not wait to see the result of a loving act to feel satisfied, seeing how this can occur much later and not in our immediate perspective. The loving intention does have an immediate effect on the person it is directed to, but it will be facilitated by the need and the merits accrued to that person. Then, God's time frame and judgment will guarantee the expected result. A loving effort is never wasted, but the results can be unexpected for the one who makes it.

If our actions are offered as a deal with God, where we expect special benefits for our results, this will not be a loving action but a selfish one, which does not help neither giver nor recipient.

## EXERCISES TO INTERNALIZE THE MESSAGE

Begin with the Meditation of the Colorful Bath of Love. (See References and Resources.)

Review your life and try to find experiences where your loving intentions did not have the expected result, and think of how you reacted. Then, remember the unexpected but welcomed surprises in your life that seemed to appear out of nowhere. Were they merely luck, or were they "late" results of your loving actions or those of others? The law of cause and effect is measured in the time frame of God, not of man. Also, recall how many personal plans were orchestrated by people or situations that seemed random.

# QUOTE 43

*Before knowing God, you must know yourself. Dare to do so!*

This quote, said to have been written in the Temple of Apollo at Delphi and part of the Greco-Roman mystery schools, appears to say that wisdom is hidden within our own minds. It also suggests that to discover this mystery, we must be brave. Remember quote number thirty-eight, "Our shadows seem larger when we approach the light."

This quote is like the manner of learning expressed by Plato and repeated by the Buddha: "Learning is remembering what we have already experienced." In my book, *Spirituality 103,* I maintain that we can discover our light, hidden within the darkness of our minds (the material mirror) if we understand that they are just emotional reflections created by the ego, which distort the beautiful and pure image of the son of God in our minds. Remember that we are a creative reflection in the Magical Mirror, or mind of God. To look at the reflection of our own mirrors is a daunting process, for these distorted images and shadows were created by our emotion's unconscious (exclusive) actions, and we may not understand that they are totally fictitious since their power depends on our ignorance.

## EXERCISES TO INTERNALIZE THE MESSAGE

Begin with the Meditation of the Colorful Bath of Love. (See References and Resources.)

The most effective exercise to discover the light hidden in our shadows is the key to forgiveness, wherein we comprehend that they were created because our disconnection from the light obscured us in the solitude of the ego and its emotions, which imprisoned us in a mental jail within our subconscious. The process of forgiving our incapacity to understand those lessons of love at that moment is the quickest form of freeing ourselves from this prison. It is important to note that the Creator does not blame us for erring with our free will.

# QUOTE 44

*Patience and compassion are born from the wisdom learned from our mistakes.*

To understand the meaning of this quote, we must first study the origins of the words patience and compassion.

Patience is the balance between attitude and the capability to overcome difficult situations and conflicts. It is characterized by those who act with tranquility, which is to say, one who does not lose their calm, no matter the adversity of their reality. It is generally related to bravery, maturity, and perseverance, and comes from the Latin word "patis," meaning "suffering."

Compassion is a word that comes from the Latin word "cumpassio," meaning "suffering together." It is a human value, where one can comprehend the situation of another, and connect with them with empathy in spontaneous solidarity to help them.

We can, therefore, conclude that these qualities are inexorably linked by a common thread of suffering, when sympathy and empathy allow us to understand the sufferer as if we were the ones in their shoes. This usually happens upon remembering a similar situation. First, we must remember how that experience generates compassion, and then how we overcame that situation. That is why our lessons of love, or mistakes, make us more compassionate and patient. The following quote comes to mind: "Let any one of you who is without sin be the first to throw a stone at her" (John 8:7). Yet, we should not confuse pity with compassion, for with pity, the observer does not understand the experience of the one who suffers, for he cannot think it can happen to him or her.

## EXERCISES TO INTERNALIZE THE MESSAGE

Begin with the Meditation of the Colorful Bath of Love. (See References and Resources.)

Review your life and recall when your juvenile attitude of feeling immortal and invulnerable began to change. Why did we have to wait to suffer in order to become sensitive to the suffering of others? Remember the common saying, "Nobody learns in a foreign mind." We cannot be selfish; we must focus our efforts on inclusive actions which have loving results in us and in all the children of men that we share the universal experience with. Practice the key to forgiveness, and find the hidden lesson in the exclusive or selfish actions in our lives.

# QUOTE 45

*We must read the story of our life without skipping the difficult and tedious parts if we wish to understand and accept its inevitable end.*

Only in the fantasies described in fairy tales and cartoons are there always happy endings. There is no story, be it human, familial, religious, or scholarly, where there is no contrast between happy moments and unfortunate ones.

Although, from our external point of view, the lives of others are filled only with positive experiences, so we can never know how they perceive it from their own perspectives. The beings that already learned to confront their lessons of love with a "what for?" and not a "why?" always maintain a smile and hopeful attitude throughout their lives, which allows them to see their end as a happy one.

No part of our story is out of place or unnecessary, and therefore we must have the patience to live fully through each one of these parts without skipping the page.

## EXERCISES TO INTERNALIZE THE MESSAGE

Begin with the Meditation of the Colorful Bath of Love. (See References and Resources.)

We must review all the parts that were skipped in our stories in order to find the lesson of love hidden within that we did not understand at that moment. We will find the hidden wisdom in all of them via the forgiveness code. We must also help our loved ones, using our own experiences of love, to never skip the unpleasant parts of their own lives.

# QUOTE 47

*Free will implies the great responsibility of choosing and facing the consequences of any action taken.*

Free will is a privilege, which allows us to responsibly choose from the multiple directions our capabilities can take us, using the inclusive motivation of the Golden Rule to face the consequences of these decisions. This privilege is not a free pass for irresponsible debauchery based on exclusive and selfish motives. The law of love, or the law of cause and effect, rapidly balances those selfish acts with new and varied lessons of love so we may understand their irresponsible consequences.

## EXERCISES TO INTERNALIZE THE MESSAGE

Begin with the Meditation of the Colorful Bath of Love. (See References and Resources.)

By reviewing our history, we see how many of our exclusive actions, done under our freedom to act, brought us very painful repercussions that filled us with guilt and remorse. We must understand that free will is not entirely free, nor can it be equal, for it must vary with age, capacity, education, economic situation, and gender. That I may learn to play an instrument or sing a melody does not guarantee I can play in an orchestra or sing in an opera.

# QUOTE 48

*God created us to spread a mass epidemic of love across His creation. What have you done today to infect others?*

The sons of man love when others solve their problems and take their places during the exams of life, only for them to take credit for the results. Some like to resolve the issues of others following their own criteria, again expecting praise for the ensuing success. These are known as co-dependencies, and in my previous book, *Spirituality 101,* I call them spiritually lame. One uses another as a cane, tying together the weak "victim" and the stronger "victor" to a common shackle, as if they were Siamese twins that cannot make decisions independently from one another.

These codependent relationships also occur between the children of man and God, where the children want God to solve all their problems, only to shift the responsibility onto others when they are not addressed, blaming the devil or even God. They do not understand the purpose of Creation, and the creative responsibility man shares with God. The only way that the love of God can be manifested in its creation is via his beloved children, as it happened in the life of Jesus. Every one of us carries the seed of love like an infectious virus that we can easily spread to others.

## EXERCISES TO INTERNALIZE THE MESSAGE

Begin with the Meditation of the Colorful Bath of Love. (See References and Resources.)

Let us remember how someone infected us with love for the first time. Let us recall how we have infected others. One of the most viral methods is a smile, and another is a hug. Sometimes lending an ear without judgment or gossip is another form of contagion. By extension, giving testimony of the similar weaknesses suffered during bad experiences can be a way to spread the pandemic. Finally, forgiving acts of exclusivity and selfishness is yet another way to spread the contagion.

# QUOTE 49

*Do not respond with your shadow to the warrior of shadows; answer with your light so that you may help him discover his own.*

This is one of my favorite quotes, previously shown in my book, *Spirituality 103: The Forgiveness Code*, where the focus is an imaginary battle between the warriors of light (children of God) and the warriors of shadow (children of man). Here, the shadows are dragons created by emotional hardships that distort the pure, original image of the warrior of light, as reflected in the Magic Mirror (mind) of God. These shadows are legendary monsters birthed by negative emotions and begotten by selfish acts, which proceed to haunt us throughout our lives.

These shadows live in the deepest part of our subconscious, from where they attack subliminally in dreams as well as when we are awake. Their reign is the sinister darkness of exclusivity and ego, wherein the light of love does not exist. The sons of man, or the warriors of shadows, guided by their blind ego, march to mental battles where they attack each other with their shadows, which only reinforces them and creates more shadows for them to fight. The only way to appease these warriors is to bring the light of love to their subconscious prisons so they may begin to find the perfect, beautiful image of the warrior of light they really are.

## EXERCISES TO INTERNALIZE THE MESSAGE

Begin with the Meditation of the Colorful Bath of Love. (See References and Resources.)

Recall how all interactions, be they social, familial, marital, work-related, or religious, were hindered by the emotional interactions between the shadows of everyone involved. Recall how fear, anger, envy, jealousy, grudges, hate, and other negative feelings birthed a rupture in the loving communication between all relevant parties, fanning the emotional fires to dangerous heights. Recall, too, how the sons of man seemed to transform into beings that were irrational, insensitive, and violent, which appeared more and more like the grotesque monsters in your shadows.

Also observe how the effects of alcohol and drugs, both illicit and prescribed, promoted these battles with your shadows and those of others.

# QUOTE 50

*Life is a journey where the goal is not your destination, but the experience you obtain on the way there.*

In all leisurely trips that are done at high speed (such as by train or plane), if we only appreciate the journey's end, we cannot claim to know the entire country. If we have not traveled it slowly, by foot or car, going through the back alleys and villages and meeting the people who live there, we have not appreciated the full experience said voyage offers. My favorite trips have been the ones where I don't use maps, and I go off the beaten path I'd planned (or was planned for me) as a tourist.

## EXERCISES TO INTERNALIZE THE MESSAGE

Begin with the Meditation of the Colorful Bath of Love. (See References and Resources.)

Those who dedicate themselves to traveling the recommended tourist routes end up staying at "all-inclusive" hotels, which further limit the experience to traditional major attractions (which, inevitably, are similar to the ones you can find in your homeland). Remember that, even within our own countries, we can continuously discover new and exciting spots without spending so much money, only by wandering off the most-traveled paths.

# QUOTE 51

*Satisfying a hungry man is simple; satisfying an ambitious one is impossible.*

This quote relates to what satisfies a man, following the need he is trying to satisfy. There are basic, physiological needs that we need to fulfill, much like all living beings. However, the emotional and mental needs—the ones that do not occur in animals—are harder for us to satisfy. A bounty of knowledge, political power, youth, and outer beauty can partially and temporarily satisfy those who envy others who have fulfilled their basic needs. But ambition can never be satisfied; if he sees others who are more successful or wealthy, he becomes envious.

For that reason, mankind's spiritual void can never be filled by material gains or wants, no matter their assigned value. Ironically, the only way to satisfy the ambitious man is by satisfying the lack of love in their soul, which has lingered since they forgot their origin of light. This is something that others cannot help with, for each one of us must find spiritual fulfillment within our own hearts.

## EXERCISES TO INTERNALIZE THE MESSAGE

Begin with the Meditation of the Colorful Bath of Love. (See References and Resources.)

Review how you have sought to satisfy different forms of hunger and how, by solving them, new ones appeared that were impossible to fill. Recall how, while improving your social and economic situation, you found yourself developing more ambition and finding less satisfaction with the rewards. Review your eating habits, cars, social groups, your school (as opposed to the one you send your children to), and your vacationing habits, and you will find how you were never satisfied.

Now, remember how your ambition grew more and more voracious over the years. Think if you changed your vision at any point and decided to search for the hidden manna that beats within your soul. If you exercise your key to forgiveness, you can progressively mitigate the hunger of ambition with empathy and compassion, born from learning to share the creation with all our brethren of light.

# QUOTE 52

*The Master is nothing more than a disciple who likes to help others find their mastery.*

For a long time, my concept of "teachers of spiritual matters" was falsely glorified by the historic descriptions of the great teachers of various religions and their saints. The stories of their lives were filled with many miraculous experiences and superhuman actions, which elevated them, in my eyes, to a pedestal unreachable by the average person. This made me feel incapable of imitating them in daily life.

It was not until I began to revise the lessons of love I learned throughout my own life that I could appreciate the mastery of those special beings who supported me during difficult experiences with their patience and compassion, without boasting their own achievements and qualities. This shows that, contrary to my earlier views, these people are exemplary due to their childlike simplicity and the lessons learned from their innate wisdom, patience, and compassion with our mistakes.

As the saying goes, "The road is made by walking." The teacher earns his degree by learning and teaching, continuously, an endless chain of love and compassion in the school of life. There is no greater satisfaction than seeing how our students exceed us in their actions and experiences, learning from us, and surpassing our achievements.

## EXERCISES TO INTERNALIZE THE MESSAGE

Begin with the Meditation of the Colorful Bath of Love. (See References and Resources.)

First, recognize all the people who lovingly offered you their wisdom with examples and testimonies. Then, perform an exercise of thankfulness for each and every one of them, and commit to continue to share the knowledge we learn from within. Understand and forgive those who, with their negative examples, distanced you from selflessness and humility.

# REFERENCES AND RESOURCES

## MEDITATION OF A COLORFUL BATH OF LIGHT

(Meditation of the Warrior of Light from chapter eight of the book *Spirituality 103, the Forgiveness Code: Finding the Light in Our Shadows* by Iván Figueroa-Otero, MD)

Seated in a comfortable position with our back straight and our head held up high, let's visualize, in our mirror, a source of spiritual strength or energy that makes us feel protected. For example, visualize the figure of the Warrior of Light or any preferred religious figure who is young-looking, smiling, and standing with open arms and beaming rays of multicolored light from the center of his heart to ours, in which a mirror with a small seed exists.

Let's understand the meaning of the exercise. The warrior represents the human manifestation of the light, which is the force of love that it reflected from its Magical Mirror so that we could know the immensity of its creation. The multicolored rays represent the infinite ways in which love may manifest, or reflect, among us. The seed in our heart represents the passive form of the warrior of light that dwells in the warrior of shadows.

As those rays of light fill our heart-mirror, we can feel ourselves loved and protected by love, and we can observe how the small seed starts to open and, in turn, beams these multiple colors of love in all directions. Let's first imagine that those colors bathe us in loving light and penetrate every part of our bodies, especially those where there are some emotional scars, and let's see how these are soothed and healed.

After we are filled with happiness and wellness, we're going to share this with all other warriors, especially with those who have hurt us due to their ignorance of their light.

Let's visualize multicolored rays beaming from our heart-mirror towards all warriors without distinction, including those who have left this world and those that, according to us, have brought suffering to our lives. Let's dedicate a few minutes to this action, and then let's rest our mind in silence for a few more minutes. Let's finish by giving thanks for this opportunity. Let's do this exercise every day upon waking and when going to sleep.

Finally, to keep our mind in a peaceful state, let's imagine that our thoughts are like clouds in the sky and that our natural, peaceful state is like the blue color in the sky. Let our thoughts pass like clouds without following them, focusing on the blue of the sky, our natural state.

## LIST OF REFERENCES

Books that helped me craft my vision, either directly or indirectly:


- The Bible
- *Door To Inconceivable Wisdom and Compassion* by Khenchen Palden Sherab and Khenpo Tsewang Dongyal
- *Opening to Our Primordial Nature* by Kenchen Palden Sherab and Khenpo Tsewang Dongyal
- *El Ser Uno* (6 tomos) by Franca Canónico, found at https://www.elserunobooks.com/
- *Tao Te Ching* by Laozi
- *The Holy Zohar* by Shimon bar Yochai
- *El Kybalion* by Tres iniciados
- *La Autobiografía de Un Yogi* by Paramahansa Yogananda
- *Los Diálogos* by Platón

- *The Self-Aware Universe* by Amit Goswami, PhD
- *A Brief History of Everything* by Ken Wilder
- *Cutting Through Spiritual Materialism* by Chogyam Trungpa
- *The Road Less Traveled* by M. Scott Peck
- *Siddhartha* by Hermann Hesse
- *The Guide to the Bodhisattva Way Of Life* by Shantideva
- *The Tibetan Book of Living and Dying* by Sogyal Rinpoche
- *Love Is Letting Go of Fear* by Jerry Jampolsky
- *Illusions* by Richard Bach
- *The Relaxation Response* by Dr. Henry Benson
- *A Course of Miracles* by Helen Schucman
- *Quantum Healing* by Deepak Chopra
- *The Prophet* by Khalil Gibran
- *BioÉtica: La Medicina Natural, Una Alternativa Moderna* by Dr. Norman González Chacon

# ABOUT THE AUTHOR

## IVÁN FIGUEROA-OTERO, MD FACS, FAAMA

After graduating from the University of Puerto Rico's (UPR) School of Medicine, Dr. Figueroa-Otero worked as a general surgeon at UPR's medical hospital and integrated a one-year fellowship in the study of cancer and one year in experimental research and clinic. Post-graduate studies in pediatric surgery at Miami Children's Hospital and San Juan Municipal Hospital followed.

Looking for non-surgical or less invasive options for pediatric conditions, Dr. Figueroa-Otero explores Eastern philosophies that emphasize a holistic approach. He was one of the first physicians to become certified in medical acupuncture in Puerto Rico, training in traditional Chinese medicine and acupuncture with professors from the University of Seville. Eventually, he was certified in medical acupuncture nationwide.

In 2009, Dr. Figueroa-Otero achieved a certification in anti-aging medicine. In December of that year, he retired from the practice of pediatric surgery, focusing instead on a comprehensive medical practice emphasizing disease prevention and modifying lifestyles. In 2011, he was invited to become a trustee of the American Board of Medical Acupuncture, which is the national body responsible for certifying physicians in the field of acupuncture through national exams. In that same year, he was recognized by *Natural Awakenings Magazine* as the holistic physician of the year.

Currently engaged in his private practice, Dr. Figueroa-Otero continues in his role as an educator, trying to achieve full integration of traditional Chinese acupuncture courses in the curriculum of medical schools, as an advocate for allowing the physicians to be certified both locally and nationally, and as an advocate for establishing clinical research protocols on the use of acupuncture in known conditions compared to the methodology established by modern medicine. Another immediate priority of his is to incorporate meditation techniques in preventive and therapeutic medicine treatments.

Dr. Figueroa-Otero is the author of the School of Life series, with his previous books: *Spirituality 101: For the Dropouts of the School of Life*, *Spirituality 1.2: For the Disconnected from the School of Life*, and *Spirituality 103: The Forgiveness Code.* His books received awards such as the Benjamin

Franklin Award, NIEA Award, Readers' Favorite Award, Beverly Hills Award, and USA Best Book Awards. The books have also received great reviews by *Focus on Women Magazine* and the *Kirkus Book Review*, among others.